From My Self To My Savior

Ellen Myers

The Providence Project
Whitewater, Kansas 67154 USA
www.providenceproject.com

FROM MY SELF TO MY SAVIOR

PRODUCED IN THE UNITED STATES OF AMERICA

ISBN 1-59057-012-X

Contents

Foreword

Beginning in the 1970's and continuing for about twenty-five years, my mother, Ellen Cremer Myers, wrote the memoirs which follow. Sometimes she would give us children eight or ten pages at Christmas, sometimes just a page or two, and sometimes a few years would pass between "installments." This is why there is occasional repetition in her accounts; it was helpful to set the context anew as she returned to an event that she might have written about years earlier. It is also why her memoirs are not always in chronological order.

As we children have reached middle age, we have appreciated more fully what Mom's life has meant, not only to us, but to so many in the Wichita, Kansas area, across the entire state, and even throughout our nation and overseas. I'm not sure who first suggested that we should put Mom's memoirs together in book form, but it seemed like a really good idea. And, as it has turned out, this pleasant job has become mine, along with the help of two of our daughters, Anna and Hosanna. I have collated Mom's memoirs so as to facilitate the flow of her story, with occasional editing to smooth some transitions. Occasionally, I have inserted a number in brackets near the beginning of a paragraph to indicate the year in which Mom wrote what immediately follows.

Mom continues to keep busy in so many ways—volunteering at church, conducting a ladies' Bible study, writing, and teaching homeschool students, to name just a few. Her mind is sharp, her health is strong, and, as she enters her eighties, her involvement stretches the limits of some of us in our fifties! One of Mom's deepest concerns is her burden for persecuted Christians around the world. Mom now serves as Area Representative for Voice of the Martyrs (VOM), and speaks in churches, schools, and civic meetings. To contact VOM, write P.O. Box 443, Bartlesville, OK 74005, or call 918-337-8015.

Mom, you have been such a blessing to Ken, Karen, Mark, Christie, John, Becky, and me! We love you, and thank the Lord for all that He has worked in our lives through you.

Edwin C. Myers (child #2)
Whitewater, Kansas

Dear Ones,

I WRITE down *[1977]* what follows in bits and pieces, as I would remember and tell it to you over one of our big meals around the dining room table. You have asked often that I preserve my memories for you. At first I felt self-conscious—why preserve glimpses of *my* life? Next, I pleaded other work—why do *this*, when so much else needs doing? I'll do it when laid up with a broken leg, I told someone—for how could I sit still long enough otherwise?

Then, finally, I began to see it as *fun*—as our Lord's blessing, for me simply to enjoy. I have had a wonderful, adventurous, action-packed life! Every moment always mattered intensely. No greys in my vision—it all was black and white, or of vivid color. Every morning was marvellous, for what great adventure might not this day bring? What new unique human being might enter my life? What great work might demand my total energy, ingenuity, and perseverance? What fascinating new thing might be learned, book read, or melody heard!

Of course, now it is all twice as wonderful, a million times as wonderful, because now I recognize in it all the providence of our Joyous, Glorious, Almighty and Wonderful Father God. He also is *intense!* With Him also there is *no indifference, no dullness; He is life and love Himself.* In HIM *already now* all error, perplexity, anger, grief, misunderstanding in and between His children simply dissolves, is less than nothing, is swallowed up in victory, newness of life, joy, peace.

When I became new in Christ, my past, too, was redeemed. And, so redeemed, I share it with you all, with love, as He recalls it to me.

Your mother, grandmother, great-grandmother, and friend—

Ellen Myers

Before I Was There

MY father, Dr. Carl Cremer (pronounced "Kramer"), was born in Essen, Westphalia, Germany, on May 10, 1876, the first son of Judge Carl Cremer and his wife Anna (née Schulze-Vellinghausen). They had three other children. Everyone told me that my grandmother was one of the best Christian women they had ever known! She died when I was in my second year, so I have no memories of her at all. My grandfather survived her by only a few months, I believe. "He did not want to live on alone," my parents told me. My mother had only praise and memories of my grandmother's kindness and love. I was also told I resemble her a little.

Grandmother Cremer's maternal grandfather, Gerdes by name, was a young man of military age in the Napoleonic wars. At that time, when you were called up for service, you could pay someone else to take your place—a so-called "remplaçant." Grandfather Gerdes' folks found a remplaçant—and he never returned. Had Grandfather Gerdes gone to the war himself, I might well have never been. Long before I became a Christian, I would wonder at this chain of circumstances which had to "happen" for me to exist.

When my father was a boy, his family moved to Hagen/Westphalen. Pursuant to my grandfather's wish, my father studied law (he would have preferred history) at the University of Tuebingen. His final examination grade was insufficient for him to be appointed a judge, so he began to practice law instead. He also ran for state representative in the Prussian "Landtag," or state legislature, as a member of the "National-Liberale Partei," and was elected more than once.

Some years before World War I, my father married Hilda Funke, from Hagen. They had no children. My father was in office when World War I started, and he resigned to enter military service. Almost immediately he was severely wounded (shot through both thighs) at the famous Battle of the Marne (September 1914). He was treated and then sent to the Polish area occupied by Germany to serve with the German Military Government there. While my father was serving in the War, Hilda met a German Jewish dentist. Hilda divorced my father, married this man and made her home with him in Munich. I never knew what she looked like. However, my father had been very fond of her father, Geheimrat or Justizrat Funke, and kept a photograph of him on his desk.

My father, Carl Cremer, as a young man, 1896

It was during the War, while my father was serving as commanding officer of the German military government offices in Byalistok, Poland, that he met a young Polish nurse, Miss Ruchla Ruslender. Some years afterward, she and my father were married in Germany, and so it was she who later became my mother, Dr. Maria Cremer.

My mother was born into a Jewish family in Warsaw, Poland, on November 22, 1893. Her father's name was Abraham Ruslender, her mother's maiden name Anna Engelscher. "Ruslender" means "from

Russia," while "Engelscher" means "English." I like that—even the very names of my grandparents are international.

My mother had an older brother, my Uncle Leon Ruslender, who came to the United States before World War I and lived for many years in Washington, D.C. with his wife Fannie. My mother also had another brother, or perhaps cousin, who emigrated to San Francisco.

My mother also had at least two other brothers and two sisters, all of whom were killed during the Holocaust together with their families; the only one who escaped, to my knowledge, was the son of one of my mother's sisters whom I met after World War II. His name was Ignace ("Jack") Ozarow. The last I knew he lived with his wife Helen and two daughters in Maryland. According to my mother's rare references to her family, her parents both died before the time of the death camps.

My mother went to school in Warsaw. At that time Poland was under the rule of Russia, and Russian was still the official language in schools. My mother thus grew up speaking Polish and Russian, and, I suppose, Yiddish—at least she knew songs in Yiddish. I well remember her singing the Yiddish song, "Auf dem Pripetchok brennt a Feierl, in die Stub ist kalt," which Steven Spielberg used in the famous movie "Schindler's List." Later she also learned German, which she spoke so well that no one even guessed that she was not born in Germany. She also knew some Czech and French, but not Hebrew.

Her family was not religious, but, in fact, determinedly agnostic, as are so many modern Jews. They experienced the hostility against Jews that was rampant among Poles and Russians. The Russian Orthodox called Jews "Christ-killers" and periodically instigated "pogroms" (riots) against Jews. Once when my mother was four years old, there was a "pogrom" by Cossacks upon the Jewish quarter of Warsaw, in which her home was broken into. She told me how she hid under a bed and kept very, very quiet so that no one would find her and maybe kill her. (The movie *Fiddler on the Roof* is set in that time and culture, and recaptures much of what my mother's childhood and youth must have been like.) However, if Jews converted to Russian Orthodoxy, they could assimilate with Russians. (For example, Lenin's grandfather, Moishe Blank, who was Jewish, converted to Russian Orthodoxy. He adopted the name of his godfather and called himself Alexander Dmitrievich Blank. He was thus able to become a respected and moderately wealthy police physician.) This was the major difference between the times of Russian and Nazi domination: the Nazis hated Jews because of their "race," not their religion, and sought not their conversion, but their extermination.

My mother, Ruchla Ruslender, 1922

My mother studied medicine to become a nurse, and served as a nurse for the Russian army in World War I. When the Russians retreated before the German advance, my mother was left behind in a Polish town named Bialystok to tend Russian soldiers so severely wounded that they could not be evacuated with the retreating army. Then the Germans moved in and established a German military government headquarters in Bialystok, with my father as commanding Officer. This is how my parents first met. My mother already knew German well and often served as interpreter. After World War I ended, she could have returned to Warsaw, moved to Russia, or emigrated to Germany. She chose the latter, and contacted various German officers she had met, among them my father. My father and my mother were married on August 19, 1924 in Berlin after my mother had earned her doctorate (German degree: Dr. rer. pol.) in "Volkswirtschaft," i.e., political economy, or what we would call today "economics," from the University of Berlin. Shortly before their wedding, my mother left

Judaism (I don't think she ever adhered to it religiously) and was baptized into the Christian faith.

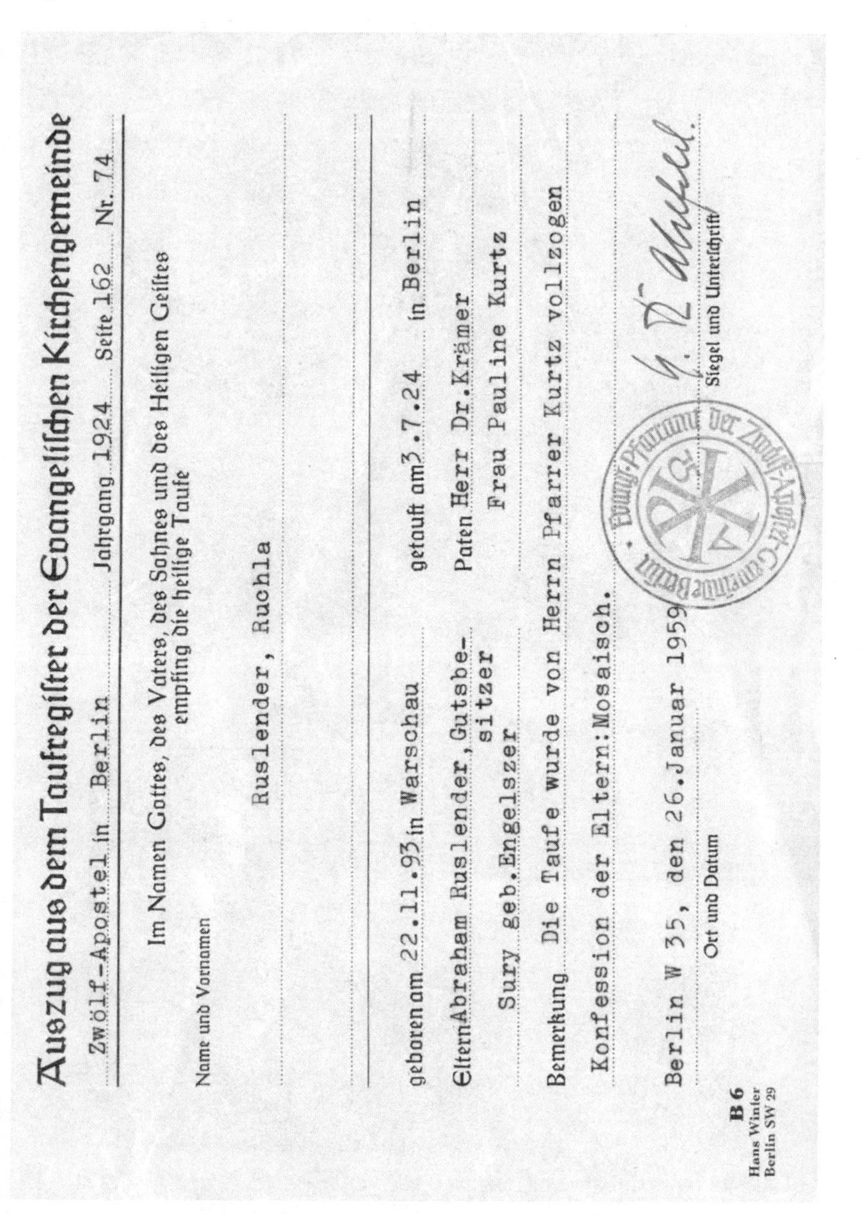

Auszug aus dem Taufregister der Evangelischen Kirchengemeinde

Zwölf-Apostel in Berlin Jahrgang 1924 Seite 162 Nr. 74

Im Namen Gottes, des Vaters, des Sohnes und des Heiligen Geistes
empfing die heilige Taufe

Name und Vornamen Ruslender, Ruchla

geboren am 22.11.93 in Warschau getauft am 3.7.24 in Berlin

Eltern Abraham Ruslender, Gutsbesitzer
Sury geb. Engelszer

Paten Herr Dr. Krämer
Frau Pauline Kurtz

Bemerkung Die Taufe wurde von Herrn Pfarrer Kurtz vollzogen

Konfession der Eltern: Mosaisch.

Berlin W 35, den 26. Januar 1959
Ort und Datum

Evang. Pfarramt der Zwölf-Apostel-Gemeinde Berlin

Siegel und Unterschrift

B 6
Hans Winter
Berlin SW 29

A copy of my mother's Certificate of Baptism

My parents were married in the Kaiser Wilhelm Gedaechtniskirche in Berlin, part of the German Reformed Church. Years ago, I had a copy of John Calvin's *Institutes of the Christian Religion* in German, now lost, owned originally by my father and with remarks penciled in the margin by my mother.

Mother and Father on their wedding day in Berlin, August 19, 1924

Auszug aus dem Trauregister

der evangelischen Kirche Zwölf-Apostel in Berlin

Jahrgang 1924 Seite 157 Nr. 48

Alle für die Abstammung wichtigen Angaben, die in dem vorbezeichneten Eintrag enthalten sind, müssen wiedergegeben werden; auf andere Einträge darf jedoch zur Ausfüllung nicht zurückgegriffen werden.

Bräutigam:	Name, Vornamen, Familienstand, Religion, Beruf, Alter (falls eingetragen, Geburtsdatum), Geburtsort, Wohnort usw. C r e m e r, Carl, früher Rechtsanwalt, Dr.jur. geb.10.Mai 1876, ev. geschieden, Berlin Bülowstr.11
	Trautag: 19.8.24.Standesamt III/ kirchl. 21.8.1924
Braut:	Geburtsname. Vornamen, Familienstand, Rel., Beruf, Alter (falls eingetragen, Geburtsdatum), Geburtsort, Wohnort usw. R u s l e n d e r, Ruchla, Dr.rer.pol.ev. geb. 23.November 1893, Jgfr.
Eltern des Bräutigams:	Name (Geburtsname der Mutter), Vornamen, Beruf, Wohnort, Angabe ob verstorben usw. Cremer, Carl, Landgerichtsdirektor, Gelsenkirchen wohnhaft

Wenden!

My parents' Marriage Certificate

Mother in 1924.

Father in 1924 (Reichstag photo)

By this time my mother's maiden name was given in the documents as "Maria Ruslender," though her original first name was "Ruchla" or "Ruhla." All who knew her as long as I can remember called her and knew her as "Maria." However, on her Jewish identity card, I.D. Number A 472 205, issued by the Polizeipraesident in Berlin, 161, Polizei-Revier ZW., signed J. K. Baumgaertner, on January 24, 1939, her first name is given as Ruhla Rachel. "Rachel" or "Sarah" were names the Nazis simply decreed to be given to all Jewish women in addition to their real names. [See later in the chapter, "Death Comes Near."] The name "Maria" does not appear on this document at all. She is also listed on this I.D. card as "without profession," although she held her earned doctorate in economics, had taught economics as a "Privatdozent" (non-tenured professor) at the University of Berlin, and regularly wrote many articles on economics for German professional journals until the Nazis assumed power in January 1933.

My mother especially resented being robbed of her profession and academic achievements, which indeed were admirable. Even before being admitted to the University of Berlin, she was required to pass the difficult German high school graduation exam called "Abitur" (baccalaureate)—they would not accept her Russian high school graduation though it was then comparable to the "Abitur." Was this perhaps anti-Semitism in disguise? My mother suspected it.

After the end of World War I, my father joined the "Deutsche Volkspartei" (successor to the "National-Liberale Partei"), moved to Berlin and ran for national office. He was elected to the Reichstag (the German national unicameral parliament) in 1920 for a term of four years, and reelected twice afterwards. In 1932 he saw that the Nazis were likely to take over Germany and did not run for reelection. During this time he also conducted a very successful law practice in Berlin.

Father was 49, and Mother 31, when I was born. As was customary in those years, my parents honored several relatives by naming me for them: Anna Maria Ellen Karin Charlotte. This was probably a good thing, as I proved to be an only child. My mother later told me she did not want me to be born on "May 25, 1925"—too many fives, it might be bad luck! "Either the 24th or the 26th would have been better," she would say with perfect seriousness. It made me regard superstition as silly at an early age.

Stillness and Splendor

BERLIN, still after 43 years *[1978]*, evokes nostalgia in me. It is not so much the city at large, which I never knew very well. Rather, it is our own neighborhood—quiet, withdrawn, private—which arises in my inner sight and in my emotions. We lived in one of Berlin's wealthiest suburbs, Zehlendorf, in the province of Brandenburg. Our address, which I remembered and would recite as a small child to visitors, sure of their compliments, was "Prinz-Handjery-Strasse 76." Nice and long, isn't it? Prince Handjery, for whom it was named, was some Hungarian benefactor—I forget just what he did for Germany to have a street in Berlin-Zehlendorf named after him. But I liked the foreign name, the sound of it, the taste of elegance and authority that clung to it.

Prinz-Handjery-Strasse was a dead-end street, with huge bumpy cobblestones over which a few cars hobbled their way to the far-apart residences along its five or six blocks. The residences were surrounded by park-like gardens. Many had hedges made of clipped evergreens to seclude them further within their quiet, dark privacy. Besides such a hedge along its front border, our house also boasted tall evergreens around its corners on the east.

The house at Prinz-Handjery-Strasse 76
in Berlin-Zehlendorf

Our house was huge, three stories and full basement. I have attempted to count its rooms, and the count runs to over twenty, not including utility rooms. For an only child it was paradise, and each room held mysteries. You could leave some of them alone for a while, and visit them again much later, and notice the subtle or more evident changes, or remember the almost-forgotten pattern of the wallpaper, or an almost-forgotten painting.

Some photos from my early childhood, Berlin.

I still have several paintings from our Berlin house. One of my favorites is the little one in our dining room here, with the row of birch trees and the tiny old woman carrying a bundle of firewood and twigs.

In Berlin, it was in my father's comfortable, large study. It came down to him from his parents' home. The landscape, including the overcast sky, is that of northern Germany, and I love it. Birch trees are my favorite trees; they are not very different from cottonwood trees, so you can see why I love cottonwood trees so much. Birch leaves, also, have a joyous, merry twinkle to them as they move around in the light, just like cottonwood trees. They, too, grow well in poorer soil and wind.

The other painting I love is the large one with the fork in the road and the old barn by the wayside. It, too, portrays a northern German landscape. In Berlin, it hung over our piano in the "music room" where I spent much time. I would sit at our piano, an upright piano of black shiny ebony wood. I would softly touch a key or two—often A and C together, which makes a "minor" sound—and listen as the sound became softer and softer till I could hear it no more. "Where does it go?" I wondered. Even now, I wonder whether any sound vibration or wave ever really is "lost."

My bedroom was on the second floor, facing West. Outside the window stood a tall, skinny evergreen tree. I would daydream about climbing out the window and down that tree to go out on my own at night. I never tried to do it really, because the tree was much too far from the window. My mother's study was also on the second floor. Since my mother taught economics and political science at the University of Berlin and wrote articles for economic journals, she would seclude herself in her study and pace up and down, reciting to herself, working on her articles.

There were books and books and books—books in my mother's study, books in my father's study, books everywhere. I cannot remember where children's books were kept, but by the time I was eight there were enough of them for me also to have a not inconsiderable library, including dozens of French books. The books I loved most were historical novels about famous Christian people! All these my father must have chosen for me. In particular I remember a thick book about William of Orange, the young relative of Emperor Charles V. William became a Protestant and then seceded with his country, Holland, from the Catholic Empire. He was murdered in 1555. Even today the Dutch national anthem is of "William of Nassau," the name by which he is known there.

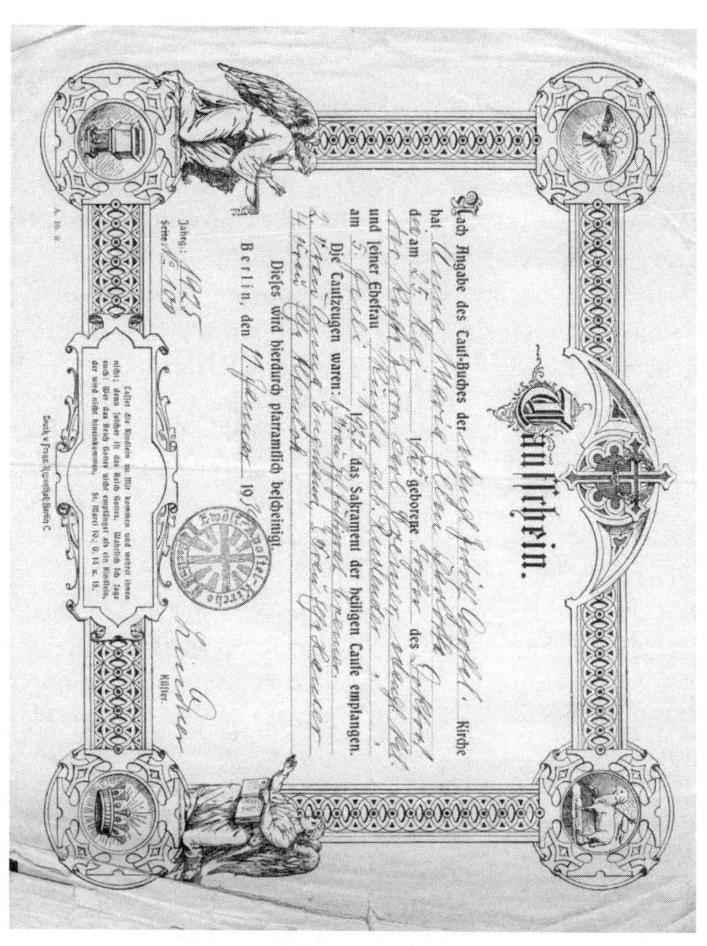
Taufschein.

Nach Angabe des Tauf-Buches der Kirche hat den am 19 geborene des und seiner Ehefrau am 19 das Sakrament der heiligen Taufe empfangen.

Die Taufzeugen waren:

Dieses wird hierdurch pfarramtlich bescheinigt.

Berlin, den 19

Küster.

Jahrg.: 1935

Seite:

Lasset die Kindlein zu Mir kommen und wehret ihnen nicht; denn solcher ist das Reich Gottes. Wahrlich ich sage euch: Wer das Reich Gottes nicht empfängt als ein Kindlein, der wird nicht hineinkommen. St. Marci 10, V. 14 u. 15.

My Baptismal Certificate

I read about the Huguenots, the Protestant Christians of 16th Century France who were finally expelled from their home country for their faith. Their leader, Admiral de Coligny, was murdered in the St. Bartholomew's Day Massacre in 1572, by instigation of Queen Catherine de Medici. Some time ago I saw a film, *The Three Musketeers*, in which the Huguenots defending their last fortress, La Rochelle, are mocked, and their defeat hailed. Even after half a lifetime, I still felt angry and myself mocked in "my" people.

It seems I was reading all the time. But I also was taken on walks, and the walks usually went to the wood that was at the end of the dead-end Prinz-Handjery-Strasse. It was a little wood, though in my earliest memory it stands out as huge and mysterious, big enough to get lost in. When I read of the beginning of Dante's great book, *Inferno,* how the poet gets lost in the dark wood, it is my little childhood wood that came back to me. When later I read one of my favorite Russian stories, "Lyes Shoomit" (The Wood is "Noising") by Vladimir Korolenko, it was also that little childhood wood I was picturing.

On the south of our house stood a great horse chestnut tree. If you have never seen such a tree, it is a pity. The chestnuts begin in the spring as huge, sweet-smelling white or pinkish blossoms. In the fall, the chestnuts will grow large and drop to the ground, still encased in their thick green prickly shells which burst open as they hit the ground. Then you can peel off the shells and extract the horse chestnut, which is shiny dark brown, so shiny you can almost mirror yourself in its lacquered surface, and with a white "underbelly," round and delicately veined. Oh, they are beautiful! These beautiful nuts, not edible, only beautiful, are another one of our Lord's joyous luxuries we cannot "use," only love, like flowers.

In the spring I would walk along Prinz-Handjery-Strasse drinking in the smell of these blooms. The foliage was thick and shiny. The tree by our house was old and tall and thick and overarched the old three-story residence so you could sit outside on the second-story balcony under its shade, and comfortably collect the chestnuts which dropped to the balcony floor in the fall.

West of our house there was the garden. In the earlier years it was "just" the ornamental garden, but a later purchase added a plot directly west of it for growing vegetables. I never quite liked the vegetable part; but my father set aside in it a little plot, maybe 5 feet by 5 feet, for me to grow whatever I wished. What I wished was carnations, and for one or two years in the early '30s I did have this beautiful little patch of red and red-and-white carnations in the middle of cabbages and Swiss chard. I can see my carnations as I write this. I don't remember picking any—just going out and keeping company with them.

But my nostalgia—a longing to see once again that which I loved long ago—is strongest in November here in Kansas. The sun, low in a sky partly overcast with greyish clouds, looks like "my" sun back in Berlin when I was a little girl. I would sit at a window in our big old house and look out and dream of walking "out there" on some straight and shadowy road in the fall country. I would leave some village behind and walk on, setting my face into a wind blowing at me through the trees bare in the fall. I would look up from time to time to see bits and wisps of clouds alternately covering and revealing the afternoon sun. I would go on to some destination—perhaps another village, or a castle set high on a hill—a hill that stood alone in a plain, never a hill among other hills, never many mountains, just one solitary hill, straight ahead, strange and awesome when all else was flat country.

It was in no way frightening, but on the contrary, full of a quiet joy. And "they" would be expecting me in that village or that castle where I was going. I would reach my destination before dark. I never daydreamed of wandering out in the country alone in the dark. The sun would set *after* I reached my destination, my "home." I dreamt this frequently while growing up. Only after I became a Christian did I finally understand its meaning: my destiny was not the world, but the castle of my King and my God.

I did not daydream of bright summer days, or snow. Nor did springtime really bring about this sort of imagination. No, it has been the fall—late fall, when the leaves are mostly gone from the trees, when one doesn't look for mild "Indian Summer" days any more, yet when night freezing hasn't yet set in, and when rain doesn't turn to snow yet—which is the seed-time of my imagination.

Always in my childhood daydreams, I might wander about in some strange November country alone—but never altogether lost, or altogether alone. Some would speculate about these daydreams being faithful pictures of my actual life, portraying my loneliness as an only child of older parents in that big old grey house in that quiet private neighborhood, as well as the great love and security provided by my parents. And maybe they are right. But neither my loneliness nor my being specially loved as the only child of older parents should be frowned at. Both were God's plan and providence for me. Both my loneliness and my having been loved as a child "worked for my good" (Romans 8:28), and I now accept them as good. There were times when I didn't—when my loneliness and my being loved (and hence much watched over, worried over and "fenced in") were burdens to me. No longer. Our God has made all things new; He has made all burdens into blessings.

Besides my dreaming, I was almost constantly making melodies in my mind, "new songs" which haunted me because I did not know how to capture them so I would not lose them. When I started piano lessons at age 7, learning how to write music was the greatest benefit to me. One of the earliest songs to which I wrote both words and melody went as follows:

1. Es flog ein kleines Voegelein *Wohl in die weite Welt hinein,* *Es sang ein Lied, nur ihm bekannt,* *Das hat es das Lied der Sehnsucht genannt.*	*1. Once a little bird flew* *Out into the wide world,* *It sang a song, known only to itself,* *Which it called the song of longing.*
2. Und von dem Lied ein Fluch ging aus, *Wenn ein Mensch hoeret die Sehnsucht daraus,* *Es klingt im Ohr ihm immerdar* *Und er von der Sehnsucht ergriffen war.*	*2. And a curse went out from the song,* *When a man hears the longing in it,* *It will ring in his ears evermore,* *And he will be consumed with longing.*

The third stanza, which I do not recall exactly, said that now the little bird has flown all over the entire world, and men everywhere have heard the longing in its song, and all have been seized by longing.

Even so I felt the longing, much like C. S. Lewis longs for his "island" in his autobiographical book, *The Pilgrim's Regress*. My longing was very much like a "curse" in its intensity, because it separated me from everday things. My dreams of wandering along that lonely road toward the castle on the hill were the pictures of that longing. For me, as for C. S. Lewis, the fulfillment came with Christ.

Though we must have been quite wealthy during my early childhood, even then I must have lived "from day to day," because my memories of my first seven years—before 1933—are quite sketchy. It is really funny, but for years I actually thought I had made a *decision* in the 1940's, during the fearful World War II air raids and the Jewish persecution, to live "day by day" and especially *not to think of or plan for the future*.

At age 8 in Berlin.

Christmas

NEARBY our house was a hill where we went sledding in the winter. Winter in Northern Germany comes in November. There were no sudden blizzards like here in the American Midwest, but rather a gradual transition from mysterious Fall to snowy Winter. It was all fun for me, since neither I nor my mother took care of muddy overboots, wet clothing, dirty footsteps on carpets or floors. There was "my" maid, and there were one or two other maids, and the cook, and the caretaker and his wife.

In Germany, both in Berlin and later on our farm, we celebrated Christmas on Christmas Eve, December 24. For weeks before Christmas, the house was filled with the smells of Christmas cookies and cakes baking. We have tried to duplicate most of these cookies and cakes here, but some we have never baked or found. I am thinking especially of a heavy kind of cupcake known to me in my childhood as "Liegnitzer Bomben"—made with much honey, molasses, candied fruit, spices—you'd think one such cupcake would serve for a full meal—but not in Germany! Then, on Christmas Eve, in the afternoon, my father would decorate the freshly cut Christmas tree. When I was little he would use multicolored ornaments; when I was bigger, he switched to only silvery and white ornaments, which made the tree look much more formal.

He never wanted any help with this work; I seem to remember he said that in his own childhood—the Germany of the 1870's and 1880's—his own father also decorated the Christmas tree. We had the beautiful old-fashioned Christmas tree ornaments such as Whitaker Chambers mentions with nostalgia in *Witness*: shiny glass globes, beautiful angels. Chambers says only the Germans knew how to make these. They had a homey, not-mass-produced look; they were handled with great care so they might be handed down from generation to generation. Some of ours came from my father's parents.

Also, as generations before us, we used candles on our tree—real candles, a special, narrow, short kind that came in special boxes. There were strings with candleholders and clips to attach the candles to the branches. Care had to be taken not to place the candles directly beneath a higher branch, lest there be a fire.

On Christmas Eve, as darkness began to descend, the family and our hired help would assemble. When I was little, my father would play the piano; later on, I would, and we would sing the old familiar Christmas carols—many, many more than you know, for as with all other songs, Germany abounds in Christmas songs also. Then we would go into the room where the tree stood, a picture of joy, peace, hominess, and tradition linking us to generations past, aglow with the candles, giving forth a smell of wax and pine wood, and everyone would find their place with their own gifts. My parents were always most generous with the hired help, and most thoughtful; I remember many times where the help would thank my parents, and I always remember the feeling of gratitude and having received what one had wished for. Always there were "Christmas plates" filled with nuts, oranges (costly then in Germany), sometimes dates and figs, Christmas cakes and cookies, and candy for everyone.

Then my father, mother and I would sit down in our own dining room, apart from the help, for our Christmas dinner—the traditional Christmas goose stuffed with apples, with trimmings. We did not have fruitcake or plum pudding, nor mincemeat pie or cranberry sauce, so I never quite learned to appreciate these "foreign" goodies! And in truth I cannot tell you too much of our "typical" Christmas dinners other than that there was abundant good food (and no sweet potatoes or sweet corn either—these I did not meet till coming to America), including usually Brussels sprouts right from our garden. For my mind would already be on my Christmas gifts, especially on the new book(s) or doll(s).

Every evening during the Christmas season, my father and I would snuff out the Christmas tree candles, he the high-up ones, I the ones on the lower branches. (Every German home had at least one long-handled candlesnuffer; we had two of these.) Toward the end of the Christmas season which extended through "Three-Kings-Day," January 6, little fires were wont to start in the Christmas tree as it grew dry.

The Christmas season included New Year's Eve, called "Sylvester" in Germany. To toast the New Year, we stayed up till midnight and ate doughnuts (a special kind filled with jam, like

"Bismarcks" are here) and drank a hot spiced drink which included red wine. My father would always be a little sad that evening. "Another year gone by," he would say, and not smile for a while. My mother would be in high spirits, looking forward to the new year which was bound to be better than the old! I loved our New Year's Eves because this was the one time when both my parents would be together in love and at peace, without any tension (Christmas might still savor of the pre-Christmas rush!). Unlike here in America, there were no fireworks. As you know, I have never even really accepted, much less learned to like this noisy, dangerous custom (sorry, that's how I feel about it—forgive me!). In Germany, New Year's Eve was *quiet*—usually there would be deep snow on the ground, or falling. There was peace, and a solemnity, an awe of time going by, of another milestone in life passed, of future events looming up, with their joys or sorrows.

My very first trip to Kindergarten, 1931

School Days

I STARTED school in 1931 at a private elementary school for girls. The school was run by what seemed to me to be a very old lady, Mrs. Anna Ludwig. I think she was Jewish but can't be sure. It was a one-room school with perhaps 25 students ages five through ten. I do not remember too much about it except that I was shining in geography, history, and music. I also did well in handwriting; those were the days when you really exerted yourself in beautiful handwriting. I learned the German script which no one can read who wasn't born in my generation or before. They stopped teaching it after World War II, I understand.

I received consistently high marks in composition, too, with one notable exception. I remember once in elementary school, perhaps 1933, when our teacher asked us to write a composition about the topic, "The Time When I Was Afraid." It was the one time in my whole life when I got an F. That's partly why I remember it, I am sure! I simply had never been "afraid." I couldn't imagine what it might feel like—I couldn't write about it at all. I was never afraid in early childhood, not even after the Nazi times began (fear only came later). I remember, half with laughter, half with amazement, that other children, who normally received F's, got A's on this composition. To them, fear was very real and easy to describe.

There have been experiences of fear later in my life. But even these experiences did not imprint themselves upon my imagination or my daydreams. I have always deliberately pushed away daydreams of future horrible happenings—except in one period of my life, the months immediately preceding my conversion to Christ. Then the very daydreams and "what if?" imaginings were part of His "grace that taught my heart to *fear*"—so grace could relieve my fear forever.

In 1934 I passed a special examination of skills and "intelligence." It was in the midst of winter, and I was sick and feverish with the mumps. But my mother insisted with great urgency on my taking this test *now*, as though my life literally depended on it. I accordingly went to the exam all bundled up, my throat swollen and aching, feeling very hot and awkward—I remember the occasion very well. The examiner was an old gentleman with snowy white hair and beard and dark-rimmed glasses by the name of Dr. Kindermann. I immediately liked and trusted him. It turned out that I was the very last candidate he examined before his retirement.

The examination was for the purpose of "jumping a grade"—Grade 4 by our reckoning in American schools—so I could transfer immediately after Grade 3 of elementary or "Volksschule" to the German "hoehere Schule" or high school at age 9 rather than 10. I passed the examination easily.

Had I not gone in for this examination, I would have had to spend another year in grade school before going on to the "hoehere Schule." This would have postponed my graduation from the "hoehere Schule" by one year also. And it would have stopped my graduation from it. For 1942—when I graduated from the hoehere Schule—was the last year the Nazis allowed "half-Jews" to graduate from it.

So, I am very grateful for my mother's insistence that I go in for this test, mumps and all. Indeed my whole life might have been different if I hadn't. For my job after graduating from high school required high school graduation. Without that job—where I learned my foreign languages—what direction would my life have taken?

> Man's goings are of the LORD; how can a man then understand his own way? —Proverbs 20:24
>
> A man's heart deviseth his way: but the LORD directeth his steps. —Proverbs 16:9

My hoehere Schule ("high school") class of 1934
I am in the middle of the group, marked by the "X".

Father and I on my tenth birthday, May 25, 1935

In a Whirl

PRIOR to 1933, my father was a member of the German parliament or "Reichstag," which was Germany's national legislature—a sort of combined Senate and House of Representatives. He was head of the Finance Committee, and a personal friend of Gustav Stresemann, one of the better-known German chancellors. Stresemann pursued conciliatory policies towards Germany's enemies during World War I and co-authored the conciliatory Rapallo Treaty, together with the French chancellor, Briand. There were some 34 parties in the Reichstag. The party of Stresemann and my father, the "Deutsche Volkspartei" (German People's Party) was moderately "liberal" (in the *old* sense), somewhat like moderate conservative US Republicans of the 1950's. It was not a splinter party, but not the largest one either. The largest was the "Deutsch-Nationale Partei" (German National Party), and it always was the largest one right up to Hitler's takeover.

Besides his political activities, my father was an attorney, specializing in corporation law. Once in a while I would visit his office in Berlin proper. He had a beautiful office. I remember the quietness of its plush carpeting. I particularly remember his big writing desk, three big armchairs upholstered in red leather, and a Persian rug, as well as the friendly courtesy of his secretaries. I recall the name of the one who stayed on with him until we moved away from Berlin in 1935—Miss Hammes. I believe she was from Westphalia, too, like my father.

One memory that stands out from early childhood is that of the parties—big parties for many people, given by my parents. I would be upstairs, supposedly in bed asleep, but really at the turn of the stairs, looking down through the banisters. Though shivering a little in my nightgown, I was unwilling to go back to get my robe or slippers because I could not miss a moment of what was going on below: the entrance bell ringing, our maid, Lenchen, answering it and escorting guests in, then taking off their wraps and hanging them up in the coat closet (only it was open—we didn't have closets with doors in Germany)—while the people joined the earlier arrivals in our large dining room. At times there must have been twenty guests altogether. Then the serving dishes would be brought in from the kitchen.

Usually by that time my excitement was over, for the people could only be heard murmuring within the dining room, with occasional bursts of laughter, or a cough. So I would slip back into my room, into the welcome quiet and darkness, digesting what I had seen, filing it away for a future where *I* would entertain. Visions would be there of many people laughing around my table. Always I imagined it to be a joy! I would *like* these people! They would be good friends! The idea that these parties were given for "connections"—for people who could be *useful*—never at that time entered my head. When I understood after years that the people who came were often not so much friends as *important* people—people whom my parents wanted to "cultivate"—I was disillusioned, though I have never been angry or disgusted with my parents because of this. Of course, my father's political career, my mother's professional career, demanded such "business entertainment." But I—I longed for *friends*.

And who would be my very best friends? Why, my children! I would have many children. I remember this from very early on also, from a time when we had not yet moved to the farm. I would daydream about my big family, my boys and my girls well-fed all around my big table, and then all snug and safe and warm in upstairs bedrooms in a big old-fashioned house. My husband was sort of hazy—of course, he would be my children's good Daddy. Perhaps like my own father, who was absent from home all day and only came home right before it was time for me to go to sleep, but who came home early on Saturdays, took me out to lunch, and then spent hours playing with me. But the children—they were all-important. I would feed them... You wonder why I just love to have a lot of people around our table? It's our Lord's fulfillment of childhood wishes, and it is every bit as good as I wished—it is better because it is real.

What else can or do I now remember about little Ellen in Berlin before 1933? I had a nanny so I rarely spent time with my mother. My father always spent as much time with me as he could. On Saturdays my father returned from work early on the noon suburban train. I would go to the railway station to meet him. Once I ran up the stairs to the platform where the train arrived, slipped, fell down on my face, and hit my mouth on the stairs. A little triangular corner was chipped off one of my upper front teeth. For many years I was quite self-conscious about this "disfigurement" which others hardly noticed!

Late Saturday afternoons my father would play with me, especially with building blocks and little farm figurines, both people and animals. We would usually construct a farm we called "Gross-Nipkau" after the farm that a friend of my father's, "Uncle Engmann," possessed in East Prussia and which we usually visited in the summer. One of the little toy figurines was therefore named "Uncle Engmann," and one of the little toy dogs was his real-life dog "Troltschek." My father would always build a sort of tall chimney on our building, and when everything was finished he would puff some smoke from his cigar up that chimney so smoke rings could float out on top, giving the whole construction a semblance of life. There also was a little toy train we could arrange to chug around the "farm," and there was an elaborate toy box which could be wound up, and which featured its own tiny little train of its own running up, down, and through a tunnel. We played with them Saturday after Saturday, sharing much the same simple everyday happy stories about them week after week.

Father would also take me on Sunday morning walks at about 11 A.M. to the "Ratskeller," the tavern in the basement of the "Rathaus," (city hall) of Zehlendorf. (Such "Ratskeller" pubs used to be and perhaps still are in many, many German city halls.) There it was his habit to have one beer, which was brought in one of the usual clear heavy glass mugs, heavily foaming at the top. "Are you drinking beer with whipped cream, Vati?" I would ask, and he smilingly went along with this fiction (I believed it!). I was very disappointed when my father later let me taste the "whipped cream"! A slice of dark rye bread came with the beer, and he would give it to me to munch while he drank his beer. I honestly think my present preference for rye bread and my present dislike of any and all beer dates back to then!

The years from 1924 to 1933 were probably the happiest in my mother's life. She became more and more established in her profession, always her highest priority. She was happily married to a prominent person, and lived in a beautiful home in Berlin's prestigious suburb of Zehlendorf. She had only one child–me–though as she told me later, something went wrong at the birth and my parents could not have any more children. Then came the January 1933 Nazi takeover of power, and for twelve years my parents could no longer work in their professions, or really at all. My mother was dismissed from her university post, and publications stopped accepting her articles because she was Jewish. Her church membership did not count; the Nazis went by "race." My father was disbarred from legal practice. He had belonged to a political party opposed to the Nazis, and, worse, he had a Jewish wife whom he would not divorce. My father had retired from the Reichstag in 1932, foreseeing the political catastrophe which was about to happen. Thanks to my mother's insistence they had bought a small farm, "Schopfenhof," in southwestern Germany in 1932.

So, being deprived of livelihood in Berlin, we moved to our farm in 1935. Our official address, however, remained in Berlin under the name of one of my father's nephews, who would regularly forward mail to us. The Berlin house was leased to a Jewish doctor after our family moved to our farm. The house was not harmed during World War II and the final horrible destruction of Berlin's occupation by the Soviet troops.

The main house at "Schopfenhof," our farm in southwestern Germany.

Change

IT HURT to leave my little patch of carnations behind when we moved away from Berlin to our farm in 1935. I was supposed to have another patch in the garden of our farm, but my heart was not in it. For, the association of "a garden enclosed" (Song of Solomon 4:12), its privacy and "useless" loveliness, was destroyed by the sheer productivity of the farm garden which seemed to blame my little patch for its idleness. I did not speak of this to anyone, but even then I had not only the feeling but the words. My father, God bless him, persevered more than I, for he nurtured his own "patches" of red geraniums year after year in built-in planters at the entrance to our farm house. My mother would sometimes rail at him for "spending all his time clipping off the dead geraniums instead of working."

My father, still being lame from his World War I injury, could not do any heavy physical work on the farm. He took care of the bookkeeping and tax work, which was as involved in Germany as it is in America today. My mother, however, despite becoming more and more overweight, put in full hours in the big garden–she was a successful gardener both with flowers and vegetables–and in the fields if she was needed. This was admirable, for she did not like this work. Thanks to her foresight in having us buy the farm before the Nazis assumed power, we always had enough to eat and wear right through the increasing scarcity of World War II.

My mother was in command of several hired women: the cook, who was the wife of the farm overseer; a woman (our wonderful Lisbeth) who took care of the milking, the chickens, the pigs, and the weekly baking of perhaps a dozen huge loaves of bread; a helper in the garden, and a helper with the household laundry (then still done by hand) and the cleaning. There were usually two or three men as well, supervised by the farm overseer. During the harvest of grain and potatoes, some extra seasonal help would be hired from the village. The permanent employees lived at the farm itself (our farm house was very big, with many rooms).

Before we actually moved to the farm, we started spending our vacations there—Summer, Fall, Christmas, and Easter. Oh yes, in

Germany the school year isn't like here—no long three months stretch of vacation in the summer, only six weeks; but that's more than made up for by two weeks of fall vacation, two weeks around Christmas, and two weeks around Easter. With these vacations at the farm, I was given my very own pet duck, whom, in a burst of originality(!), I named "Weissentchen"—"Little White Duck."

Weissentchen ("Little White Duck") and I at the farm.

It was the exploits (largely imagined) of my duck that provided the basis for my first book, which I wrote when I was eight. Although this sixty-page book was ostensibly about Weissentchen, it really centered around my thoughts about justice, fair play, and perseverance.

The manuscript came complete with color illustrations by myself. Somewhere or other I suppose in those boxes down in our basement that old manuscript may still be extant. My parents thought very highly of it, especially my mother who was great at encouraging me with interest and lavish praise. In my teens I wrote several books (which were not published), including one in French—a tragic love story! Finally, I wrote the novel *Das dritte Leben* (*The Third Life*), which was published in Stuttgart in 1946.

Thus, the writing urge in me showed itself very early. I always wanted to write of facts, true history as it were; using fiction in novel form merely served to make the history personal. My second published book was *Reprobate Silver*, published by Christianity on Campus in magazine form in 1964. Later on, in the 1970s, I dropped the novel form, writing factual articles instead, especially for the *Creation Social Science and Humanities Quarterly* (published 1978-1994).

We kept in touch with all the family, and I remember my cousins' visits, especially on our farm. My father's sister, Anna, had two sons, Fritz and Hans, which I remember well. His other sister, Else, had two daughters Ilse and Anneliese. Before World War II we saw them all regularly.

I continued my schooling at the co-educational "higher school" in the little city of Neckarsulm some distance away from the farm. I did very well in school, especially in foreign languages and history. Several boys resented this so much that they would corner me and throw rocks at me during recess day after day. No one knew that I was half-Jewish, and we sought to avoid any undue attention so no one would find out. Therefore we did not complain about the boys to the teachers who were already aware that I was politically different--I was the only student in the whole school not in the Hitler Youth! (Non-Aryan "mongrels" like myself were ineligible for membership.)

When coming home from school every day, I often had to spend a half-hour or so waiting for the train which would bring me back to the railroad station of Neudenau, the little town nearest our farm. In good weather I would spend this time sitting on a bench across from the railroad station and read.

Near this bench was a little store selling paperback books, stationery, picture postcards and candy. Here I bought my very first mystery novel, translated from the English, I believe, which made me an avid reader of such stories, especially those of Agatha Christie, for many years (even yet I enjoy TV shows like "Columbo," "Matlock," and well-made movies of Agatha Christie books). Here I also bought candy from the small allowance my father gave me every week, for reading was more fun along with eating sweets (especially the good German chocolates, hard fruit candies, and peppermints).

At first, I would buy only as much as I could pay for then and there, but eventually I bought "on account" as the lady running the little store knew me well enough by now to trust me for eventual payment. After about two months I had run up a debt of one Mark and 40 pennies; it would take several weeks to pay it back.

At this time an exceptional event took place: my father came to Neckarsulm to pick me up and bring me home by car. He wanted to see the place where I usually spent time waiting for the train. The lady hailed him from the store and told him of the debt I had run up. He paid it all then and there, but told me that he would take it out of my allowance, and that I should never run up debts again. And I never did!

The Nazis called their empire The Third Reich. One of our teachers made a joke which went like this: "What comes after the Third Reich?" No one would answer. He would then say with a smirk, "The Fourth Reich, of course." Soon afterwards he was forcibly retired on only one-third of his pension. A student in my class had told his father, an ardent Nazi official, about his politically incorrect joke. The official party line dictated that the Third Reich would last forever!

I made one lifelong friend, Laura, at the school in Neckarsulm. I spent much time at Laura's home, and learned many of the beautiful German Christian hymns there. Two of these were my favorite songs. The first was WO FINDET DIE SEELE DIE HEIMAT, DIE RUH?:

Where does the soul find its home, its rest;
Who will cover her with protecting wings?
Oh, does the world not offer me a home
Where sin cannot rule, nor tempt?
No, no, No, no, it is not here.
The home of the soul is above in the light.

The second was LOBT FROH DEN HERRN, IHR JUGENDLICHEN CHOERE:

Gladly praise the Lord, you choirs of youth!
He loves to hear a song in His honor.
Gladly praise the Lord, gladly praise the Lord.
. . .
The time will come, when we, with a thousand melodies,
(O Bliss!) will praise You, our Creator,
From eternity to eternity.

Latein- und Realschule Neckarsulm
(Name der Schule)

Zeugnisse

für ~~den Schüler~~ — die Schülerin
Ellen Cremer

geboren den 25. Mai 1925 in Berlin

eingetreten am 1. April 1931 in die Grundschule. Berlin

eingetreten am 23. April 1935 in Klasse II

ausgetreten am 20. März 1940 aus Klasse VI

Vorbemerkungen.

I. Die Stufen für die Einzelzeugnisse sind:

bis 1. Oktober 1937		ab 1. Oktober 1937		ab 1. November 1938	
sehr gut	1	sehr gut	1	sehr gut	1
gut	2	gut	2	gut	2
genügend	3	befriedigend	3	befriedigend	3
nicht genügend	4	genügend	4	ausreichend	4
		nicht genügend	5	mangelhaft	5
				ungenügend	6

II. Die Zeugnisse sind jedesmal vom Vater oder vom gesetzlichen Stellvertreter zu unterzeichnen. Das Zeugnisheft darf von ihnen zu **keiner weiteren Bemerkung** oder Mitteilung benützt werden.

III. Es liegt im Interesse der Eltern, die Zeugnishefte sorgfältig aufzubewahren, da für Abschriften, die später etwa gewünscht werden, Gebühren zu entrichten sind.

Schule Nr. 101/2. Zeugnisheft für Oberrealschulen und Realschulen (1935). 0334

The cover page of my academic record book from the school at Neckarsulm.

Frühjahr 1936 | Klasse II

Gesamturteil: [illegible]

Leistungen in den einzelnen Fächern:

Religion:	sehr gut	Naturgeschichte:	sehr gut
Philosophie:		Physik:	
Deutsch:	gut	Chemie:	
Geschichte:		Zeichnen:	gut
Heimat- u. Erdkunde:	gut	Musik:	gut
Französisch:	sehr gut	Freiwillige Fächer:	
Englisch:			
Rechnen:	gut		
Mathematik:			

Leibesübungen: vom Turnen befreit.

Bemerkungen:

Schulleiter: Kugler. Klassenlehrer: Mauthe.

Gesehen der Vater oder der gesetzliche Vertreter: Kramer.

3

Nr. 101 2.

An inside page from my Neckarsulm academic record.

The third floor of our farmhouse was used for grain storage. One day when I was going up there, a mouse ran right near me. I reached out, and grabbed it by the tail. No sooner had I picked it up, than it bent its body up and bit my hand.

I did not tell anyone about it, but the next day my hand was blue. The doctor said that I had blood poisoning, and must stay in bed until I was well. As the days went by, the blue continued up my arm through one of my veins. It was several weeks before I was well again, during which time my homework was sent home for me to do in bed. I was put on a special diet, which included lots of fresh grapes. I actually really enjoyed this time, because I loved fresh fruit, and, since I didn't have to go to school, I pursued my favorite pastime for hours. Everyone wondered and puzzled over how I could have gotten poisoned, but I never told anyone about the incident with the mouse.

One interesting incident has remained in my memory more clearly than most. It happened probably in the early years of World War II. A scruffy laborer by the name of "Louis" (an unusual name in Germany) was hired, and he was an alcoholic. One time he came home from a weekend binge in the local inn, roaring drunk and in a fury, threatening everyone with a big knife. No one including the farm overseer dared confront him, but my mother did. She calmly approached him face to face, came close to him and said, "Let's talk, Louis." They walked away, alone; no one heard what was said. Shortly afterwards he came to the farm house, climbed the stairs to his room and packed his few belongings into a bundle, which he carried with him on his back as he left, never to return. My mother later reported she had convinced him to leave, sweetening the parting by giving him a modest gift of money. I thought then and still think that her physical courage was remarkable.

The Neckarsulm school stopped short of the top grades of the 'hoehere Schule.' Therefore I moved away from the farm in 1940 to take my last two years of school in Stuttgart, the provincial capital, at a school for girls only. In my free time I read serious literature and works of philosophy in German and French. In a large public library not far from my school I spent many hours poring over the works of Nietzsche, Montesquieu, Voltaire, and Henri Bergson (his works were there though he was a Jew).

Again I was the only student in the school who did not belong to the Hitler Youth. I found out that most of my fellow students were not Nazis when giving a speech in a history class on "Napoleon, Hitler, and the Unification of Europe." I said Napoleon could not unify Europe although he tried this under the internationalist banner of the French Revolution. Therefore Hitler would most likely also fail at unifying Europe, for he came under the banner of extreme nationalism. Fraeulein Haehnle, my elderly teacher, was visibly scared. She said mine was a "very interesting" speech and quickly turned to other subjects. As I was walking home after school, all the girls in my class except three—the Nazis—came after me one by one and told me how much they admired my speech, and that they were not Nazis either! I never lacked friends in those two years. Still, when we had school rallies, everyone had to wear the Hitler Youth uniform, and I was the only one without it.

In February of 1942, I passed the difficult, comprehensive "Abitur"—the final test for graduating from higher school. Graduation itself was little more than a month away. One day Fraeulein Haehnle approached me after class in the hallway, looked around to see we were unobserved and asked me, "Are you a member of the Hitler Youth?" We both knew I wasn't. She said, "You had better join, because if you don't, you cannot graduate." I thought this over. I knew I could not join--I was a half-Jew! A week went by, and she approached me again after class. "Have you joined the Hitler Youth now?" she asked. "Yes," I replied. "All right, all right, that's fine," she said and turned quickly away.

All I know is that I received my graduation certificate along with my class, but I am sure she knew I had lied. During these years I learned French, English and Latin in school, and Russian by self-study and help from my mother. After graduation I took an intensive 3-month business course in Berlin to learn shorthand, typing and business correspondence, all taught in English.

A b s c h r i f t

R a c k o w - S c h u l e n

Private kaufmännische Berufsfachschule und Berufsfachlehrgänge
Private Sprachschule
Inhaber und Leiter: Walter Rackow und Dr. rer. pol. A. Rackow
Berlin W., Tauentzienstr. 1.

Z e u g n i s .

Fräulein Ellen C r e m e r , Berufsfremdsprachlerin, geboren am 25. Mai 1925 in Berlin, besuchte in der Zeit vom 8. April 1942 bis zum 24. Juni 1942 einen Sonderlehrgang der
e n g l i s c h e n S p r a c h e .
Der Kursus umfasste in täglich acht Stunden folgende Fächer:

Satzlehre	sehr gut
Handelskorrespondenz	gut/sehr gut
Sprachgeläufigkeit	gut/sehr gut
Dolmetscherfertigkeit	sehr gut
Landeskunde	sehr gut
Engl. Stenografie	120 Silben i. d. M.
Maschinenschreiben	220 Anschl. i. d. M.

Fräulein Cremer ist intelligent und sprachbegabt. Sie arbeitete mit großem Interesse und hat den Lehrgang mit bestem Erfolg besucht.

Berlin, den 24. Juni 1942

Agnes Hutton B. A. W. u. Dr. W. Rackow.

A recommendation from the school in Berlin where I took a comprehensive English business skills course in the spring of 1942. The last paragraph reads, "Miss Cremer is intelligent and a gifted language student. She works with great interest, and has completed the course with the best of success."

And God?

MY FATHER did what he could to lead me to Christ. He did this, first of all, by his personal life. His severe wound in World War I had left him able to walk only with difficulty on a heavy cane. His eyesight grew progressively worse; by the 1940's he could read only with a magnifying glass and very heavy glasses. He could do no manual labor on the farm, nor could he work as a lawyer. Twelve years unemployed (1933-1945)! My mother had a ferocious temper and was understandably extremely worried about our future. "What will happen? What will happen?" she would ask despairingly. Yet my father was always cheerful! Over and over again he would tell my mother and me, "You must have trust in God" ("Ihr muesst Gottvertrauen haben"--I can still hear him). His Bible was always before him in his little office or by his bedside. I would chide him: "You must know that book by heart now." He would say, "I always find new things in it." It was his joy in great adversity which impressed me the most about him, and he attributed it to Christ. Since I was a voracious reader, my father gave me many biographies of Christian heroes which I remember to this day.

My father also wanted me to be confirmed in his church, the German Reformed Church. All the years on the farm we never attended church because there was no Reformed church nearby. When I moved to Stuttgart in 1940, my father arranged for me to attend the little Reformed church there. It was small, and met in a barn-like building with no paintings, no candles, no cross even. Some 40 people attended in Stuttgart, the first congregation of a Reformed Church I had ever seen, and I cannot remember *any* church services before this. I do not think we ever went.

The Reformed Church was not supported by the German government. The predominant church was the Lutheran church, or, in Wuerttemberg (the province of which Stuttgart was the capital), the "Uniierte Kirche" or "United Church." This latter church was a Lutheran-Reformed mixture—the denomination which Dr. Walther left to found of the Lutheran Church-Missouri Synod in America. The Roman Catholic church was of course also a major group. My father was brought up a Lutheran, but turned to Calvinism (Reformed Church) in his earlier years. I have a letter from him, sent to us when our oldest son, Kenny, was born, in which he states: "It is now forty years ago that I entrusted my life willingly to God's guidance..." *That*, not the denominational switch, was the all-important and blessed event in his heart.

On occasion I would argue Calvinism with him. He could never convince me that God has deliberately from all eternity created some people to be (pre)destined for hell. Sometimes he would repeat this saying, "One must be tolerant—man muss Toleranz haben." And he *was* tolerant; the Catholic priest of our village was a frequent friendly visitor to our farm; and when Ken and I were married, Ken's membership in the Methodist church was no stumblingblock for my father (though perhaps it would have been, had he known about its apostasy).

The pastor of the little Reformed community was named Hacker. He was about 30, married, with two little girls. The "ruling elder" ("Presbyter") was a Mr. Phillip Reclam, related to the owners of a large German publishing firm, and of Huguenot descent. I would have lunch at the Reclam's home every, or nearly every, Sunday. I remember him as an elderly, grey-haired, rather cold man; the lunches were stiff and formal, and I endured rather than enjoyed them. During this period I lived in a rooming house run by Catholic nuns. I would just as soon have had my Sunday lunch there also, as all other meals, because of the much greater informality, the many other people, the laughter, and the occasional piano or music performances. I suppose the Reclams felt they were doing their duty by me, and since I knew my father had arranged for this care, I did not oppose it. Except for grace before meals, I cannot remember anyone speaking of Christ—which was the German way, where "you do not discuss religion and politics." (You did not discuss politics under the Nazis anyway—too dangerous.) It was assumed the Reclams were anti-Nazi, and this assumption made us tacit fellow opponents of the regime.

What *does* one talk about in such circumstances? Why, the little nothings of everyday affairs. "How is school? How is the weather? Will it rain? We may take a trip (this weekend, this summer, next year)... I went shopping for (clothes, food, books) (this morning, yesterday, last week)..." Once in a while Mr. Reclam would talk business—not to me, of course, the 14-year old, but to some adult also present—and while I cannot recall details after all these years, I can recall in his voice, his gestures, increased warmth, animation, interest, *life*.

Church consisted of singing hymns, with an organ playing in the rear of the congregation, the collection—as usual, I understand, in German churches, with an usher extending to each person a black cloth bag attached to a long stick, into which you dropped your coins (or "pants buttons," as Germans would joke)—and finally the sermon. The sermons by Pastor Hacker were long. I have forgotten them all!

The best witness in "religious education" I received, in retrospect, was the "religion class" conducted by the Lutheran pastor in Neckarsulm in the school I attended before moving to Stuttgart. Curiously enough, such classes were mandatory and allowed by the Nazi government. That is where I picked up the basic idea of Christianity that Jesus Christ died for our sins. That is where I learned a general overview of the books of the Bible. That is where I heard Bible stories. If my father told them to me earlier, I have forgotten that too. My mother never did.

But now, in this little Reformed church, I was to be confirmed. So I attended a confirmation class, along with one other candidate for confirmation, a bespectacled, silent, shy boy whose name it seems I never learned. We met with Pastor Hacker, in the Reclams' living room, I believe, once a week for about 45 minutes for some two months, with "homework" assignments consisting of memorization of the Heidelberg Catechism, a famous Calvinist formulation of the faith, and Bible verses in support of the Catechism's points.

Unfortunately this did not work out well. While I did learn the basic Christian teachings about Christ dying for our sins to save us from them and from eternal damnation in hell, somehow I did not get along too well with Pastor Hacker. I engaged in constant theological arguments with him, priding myself on my smartness. I do not remember the details of our debates, and I thank God I don't, for what would it profit?

But I date my rejection of God and the Bible and Christianity back to that Confirmation course, and especially to one episode. This was after one class session, when Pastor Hacker and I took a streetcar toward our homes away from the Reclams' area. We were standing on the platform at the rear of one of the streetcar coaches. I was still continuing an argument begun in class, and I asked him, "Does the Bible teach that Hitler will go to heaven--unrepentant?" He looked around in fear at the many other people standing around us and said, "Some believe that the Bible teaches that everyone will go to heaven, repentant or not." "If the Bible teaches that," I answered hotly, "I want no more to do with it, or with its God!" I remember getting off the streetcar in red hot anger long before my stop, and walking home bound and determined to reject that unjust God. I never read the Bible for myself to check out what it really said.

Pastor Hacker refused to confirm me, and contacted my father who finally talked me into continuing confirmation classes without arguing with the pastor, and to be confirmed. I complied, but inwardly rejected all the teaching I had been given. In due course I was confirmed, that is: I gave the properly memorized responses to the prescribed questions one Sunday morning before the little congregation, and thus became a "member" and eligible for Communion. I continued church attendance and visiting the Reclams while in Stuttgart during World War II, sporadically as time went on, but never stopped until much later—namely, sometime in 1944 when the church was shut down. But it was all done only to avoid arguing with, or hurting, my father, to whom, perversely and incomprehensibly as I thought, this seemed important.

You may wonder about Pastor Hacker. May he have forgiven me any sorrow I caused him. He began to preach, or rather, to end his sermons with a prayer, in 1944: "I pray that God may grant the victory in this war to the *just*." This went on for a few weeks—then one Sunday morning we came to church, and it was posted "Closed Indefinitely." I learned, probably from the Reclams, that *this prayer* had caused Pastor Hacker to be arrested in the middle of the night. For a while no one including his wife and children knew where he was. It turned out eventually that he was in the notorious Dachau concentration camp, from which he was not released until the Americans occupied it in 1945. He returned to Stuttgart emaciated, his hair snow white, most of his teeth gone. What he 'should' have prayed was, "victory for *Germany*"—and one of the members of this small congregation must have reported him to the Gestapo. His wife and little girls subsisted on what the congregation gave them. It really takes very little resistance to mark one for martyrdom under Nazi or Communist tyranny. (Solzhenitsyn went to concentration camps and exile for 13 years because of an incautious word about Stalin in a private letter to a friend.)

As I said before this little church met in a plain square building with no decorations or beauty whatsoever. However, another church I passed daily on my way to and from school had beautiful stained glass windows depicting the life of Jesus from birth to resurrection. The building was always kept open, and something in me drew me in repeatedly just to walk slowly from window to window and take in the pictures. These visits were like silent, secret retreats.

One other event happened which became important much later. I lived in a rooming house where I met a lady by the name of Anna Thalheimer. She, like my father, was crippled, in her case with arthritis. She wore high boots laced up almost to her knees, probably to help her crippled feet. She earned her living climbing the stairs in high-rise apartment buildings to collect insurance premiums. To my arrogant mind she was a poor old maid to be pitied or overlooked, but I did not let her see this. While I was inwardly proud and arrogant, I prided myself on being always "nice" and "polite" on the outside. This lady, also like my father, was always cheerful, no matter how hard her life. She was also known to give or loan whatever she could to anyone who asked her.

One evening I needed some small thing and went to her room to ask for it. As expected she helped me out with a smile. Suddenly her whole way exasperated me, and I asked in irritation: "How can you always be so cheerful?" There was a large picture on her wall. It was of Jesus, very beautiful in white and red robing, a halo around his head. He sat on a hillside, sadly looking at apostate Jerusalem below, saying "How often would I have taken you under my wing, as a hen with her chicks, but you would not." Miss Thalheimer pointed at the picture with her crippled hand and said in answer to my question, "He does it." ("Er tut's.") He gave her constant joy and kindness in spite of all her troubles. I remembered my father, joyful like her, also pointing to Christ as the answer, and thought, "It's nice if you two can believe as you do, but I am smarter." But I never forgot this little glimpse of Christ.

War and Words

RECENTLY *[1977]* I read *The 25th Hour* by C. Virgil Gheorghiu. It brought back to memory the time of World War II, and especially of my writing my first published novel, *Das Dritte Leben* ("The Third Life"). I will quote the first three paragraphs of the preface I wrote in the summer of 1946 when this book was published:

> This book was written in the months from April to early June 1944. During this time I sat almost every night from 10 pm to 2 am or longer with a screened lamp, and wrote down the events told in this book immediately after having lived through them.
>
> I had to keep what I was doing a secret from everyone, with fear. When I was interrogated by the Gestapo in May of 1944, I was carrying the voluminous stack of closely written pages with me in a briefcase. As by a miracle it was saved from discovery.
>
> At every air raid alert I saw to it that above all else this manuscript would be taken to safety in the air raid shelter. During those tormenting weeks I had only one thought: to finish this work before accident or death, threatening daily, hourly, prevented me.

My novel wasn't very good. I think I should have kept to *either* total fiction *or* factual reporting! I may set down some of the experiences told in the book in these pages somewhere: my memories from the time when I worked for the Robert Bosch company in Stuttgart, Germany, as secretary-interpreter in the personnel office for foreign workers, or "Displaced Persons". We had thousands of them from all over Europe. The main groups were the French, the Russians, and probably next largest, the Italians. I soon learned Italian, Spanish, and Portuguese, modern Greek, and even a little Armenian while working there. I already knew French and Russian, and also English. Today I am still fluent in German, French, English, Russian and Spanish, but have largely lost the rest.

My Spanish was acquired during one two-week vacation, in the following manner: I was acquainted with a Madame Eve Michiels. She was a strikingly beautiful Belgian woman who, together with her husband, was in charge of one of the Displaced Persons living camps for our factory. It was Mme. Michiels who gave me a textbook for French speakers to learn Spanish from—the "Methode Assimil." I still have the book here now; this is the best method of any I know to learn a foreign language. I took it with me to the farm and studied it for eight hours or more every day during those two weeks. Then I returned to work and knew Spanish—spoke it so fluently that Spaniards would ask me what city in Spain I was from. Also, when I returned, Madame Michiels and her husband were gone—on vacation in Belgium, and they never returned! Later the Gestapo inquired after them. They were members of the Resistance. They never were found. That is why I still have that great textbook, which I still reread from time to time to keep up my Spanish.

Back to the novel, which to a large extent was autobiographical. Not only its main character, but one other as well, have the urge to tell the world about the horrors witnessed under the Nazis. I look back at myself writing it all down and approve; or rather, I know I could not help sitting up those nights, because to remain silent and passive was to forfeit what now I know is my *soul*, my identity even then unalienable to me. Rather die than not to write! The main character in the book sacrifices his life writing down what he observes, because he becomes too exhausted and dies of tuberculosis. The other important character vanishes in a concentration camp because she attempts to arouse people to active resistance.

Unrealistic? I don't think so. Simone Weil, a French woman of Jewish descent, and probably a Christian, starved herself to death in England, attempting to live on the food rations doled out to French people under Nazi occupation. In 1944, thousands, including German Christian Klaus von Stauffenberg, paid with their lives for attempting to assassinate Hitler. And my own parents risked their lives sheltering refugees at our farm, among them Wilhelm Keil, who became President of the province of Wuerttemberg-Baden after the war.

Moments in the Madness

I SOMETIMES think that, had I already been a Christian under the Nazis, I would not be alive today. I would have given that loaf of bread to the Jew sweeping the street...

It was after working hours in 1944, and I was standing at a streetcar stop across the street from the exit of Robert Bosch. Along with me there were many other people waiting for their streetcars. As we were standing there, along the street walked a man in a threadbare light grey business suit, much too large on his thin body, pushing a big broom along the curbstone, sweeping the dirt. On the left side of his coat he wore the big yellow Star of David with the inscription "Jude" (Jew). As he came closer, I could see his sandy hair, and a thick red rash on his face—a sign of malnutrition.

In my briefcase I was carrying a loaf of bread. Because of the farm I had enough to eat. I thought, "Give that man the loaf of bread." But I did not do it, because around me were all these other people, and any one of them might have been a Gestapo agent, or have betrayed me to the Gestapo. I remember we all were silent—though everyone in a crowd like this always was silent. Then my streetcar arrived. I got in. I was relieved not to have to watch the Jew any more. But I have watched him off and on in my memory ever since.

So I wrote that book, to atone for moments of cowardice and fear like this one with the Jew. But of course it did not atone—it could not replace that loaf of bread not shared, ever.

It was the memory of this Jew that came back to me on July 10, 1960, when I knew I would not have helped Jesus Himself because I was a coward. Though I did not know it then, Jesus Himself had said long before, "As you have not done it unto the these the least of my brethren, you have not done it unto Me."

"Lord, when saw we Thee an hungered...?" Why, at that street corner in Stuttgart! How could I even write the memory of it down now without His Presence and Atonement and Forgiveness?

The job I had with the Robert Bosch Company in Stuttgart from 1942-1945 was as interpreter and secretary in their personnel office for the so-called "Displaced Persons" or DP's. These were foreign workers recruited into Germany by force, or else by the alternative of starvation in their countries. There were some 10,000 such DP's employed by Bosch. Among them were several hundred workers from Greece. My first fiancé was an Armenian who came to Germany as a DP from Greece where his family had emigrated from Turkey after World War I.

One time in the Fall of 1943, my fiancé, myself, and a cousin of his were out together. This was in Stuttgart, Germany, and air raids were becoming more frequent. It was dark and, as I recall it, a raw, wintry night.

The air raid sirens began wailing. They sounded much like police sirens do here. (For the first several years after coming to America I always felt the "air raid signal" fear when I heard police sirens.) We three hurried to the nearest air raid shelter, a big basement-like cellar built underneath one of the public squares in central Stuttgart.

More and more people came in, till the place was packed. Still more people rushed in. The air-raid warden—there was an official like this, presumably a Nazi (though I am not sure, in retrospect, that they really were that), in every public air-raid shelter—called out:

"There are too many people here for safety. All foreigners will have to leave." Officials began checking people's identity cards. My fiancé and his cousin were without citizenship—Armenians who had come to Germany from Greece. I had a German identity card.

Our turn came. "You will have to leave," said the official to my fiancé and his cousin. "You can stay," he said to me. There was dead silence in the packed place, with everyone looking at us, and at a handful of other foreigners singled out for expulsion from the shelter.

My fiancé and his cousin turned slowly toward the exit. I looked at the staring crowd and held on to my fiancé's arm as I walked out by his side. No one said a word. It was pitch dark outside—blackout, no street light, no lights from tightly shaded windows. There was a great quietness. There was no further bombing.

I walked home arm in arm with my fiancé at my left and his cousin at my right. We did not speak. From time to time we looked at each other and smiled, with defiance and joy and closer fellowship all one.

Through my fiancé I had met many of the Greek workers in our factory privately and was on good open terms with them. One of them, whose first name was Dimitrios (and I can no longer recall his last name) had been denounced to the Gestapo for illegally trading food stamps. He had been put into a "Labor Education Camp," a euphemistic term for a concentration camp, for seven weeks. He was a handsome young man before going into camp. When he came out, he had lost a number of teeth; he looked sickly and very thin. He showed me the festering wounds on his palms where he had been burned with cigar and cigarette butts, and struck with sticks across the fingers.

He came to our office to ask me whether it might possible to find out the name of the Gestapo official who had ordered his arrest. Dimitrios wanted to go to this official and ask that the food stamps which had rightfully belonged to him when he was arrested be given back to him, so he could eat till the end of that month.

I gave him the name of the Gestapo official who had signed the information letter to our factory about Dimitrios' arrest and confinement. I was concerned about Dimitrios' safety. But Dimitrios felt he had to try to get his food stamps back. How else could he eat for the next two weeks or so before he would be issued the next month's ration? He had the bravery of despair, and did go to the Gestapo headquarters in Stuttgart on his risky errand.

Soon afterwards a phone call came through to our office. My boss took it and then told me to go and report to the Gestapo headquarters immediately. I walked there from the factory. With me I carried a briefcase, and in it I carried the almost finished manuscript of the anti-Nazi novel which I was then working on. I dared not leave that manuscript behind at work or even at home, for the maid there was a Nazi and possibly snooped for the Gestapo.

It was a beautiful summer day. I arrived at the Gestapo headquarters. An official with dark hair and dark-rimmed glasses sat inside a little window by the entrance. I told him I was to see Officer Y. (I don't remember his name—forgot his name almost instantly after the interrogation and never could recall it! Freudian repression at work?) "All right," the man said, "his office is on the second floor." He pressed a button. In front of me a gigantic floor-to-ceiling metallic grate slowly clattered apart. I went through the opening and up the stairway behind it. Behind me I could hear the grate slowly clanked shut again.

I went to the second floor and then through a hallway to the office of Y. I entered—it seems to me the door stood open, but I may have knocked and then been bidden to come in. To my left, a man in civilian clothing sat at a desk. In front of me stood Officer Y. He was young—no older than his early thirties, and I think really late twenties—and not too tall. His hair was that brilliant light blond color the Nazis fondly called "Nordic." His eyes were blue, his face light complexioned. He wore some sort of a grey-blue tunic over the regulation black SS trousers and the black SS jackboots polished to a shine.

Officer Y. asked me asked me to sit down at a desk I took to be his. He asked me my name. I could not answer! I could not remember! My mind was a total blank. He did not repeat the question. We just sat there looking at each other. Finally, after what seemed to me a very long time, I remembered my name and told him. I also again remembered the manuscript in my briefcase on the floor beside my feet. Suppose they searched me and of course opened and examined that briefcase?

Officer Y. asked me my address. Again I could not remember! This time there was more than sheer fear at the root of my amnesia. What address was I supposed to give? My own in Stuttgart? My parents'? And if the latter, then which one—the one on the farm where they really lived day by day or our "cover" address to which all mail was sent, in Berlin? In the end I gave him my Stuttgart address and the address of my parents in Berlin.

Then he went to a side door in the office and opened it. He went into the adjacent room and instantly returned, pushing and kicking Dimitrios in front of him.

"Now talk to him in Greek and go over what you told him and what he told you this morning," he said.

So I repeated our conversation about the food stamps with Dimitrios in Greek step by step just as we had done that morning. Dimitrios agreed verbally with everything I said, also in Greek.

"All right," Y. said. "That checks out. You should not have told him about me. Let this be a warning to you! This time you may go. But if your name ever comes up before us again, it will be different."

I left the office and walked down the stairs. The man by the entrance either saw me coming, or maybe he had been informed by other means that I would be leaving, for, as I approached the metal grate at the foot of the stairs, it opened up before me and I walked through and on outside, free once more. My precious briefcase was in my hand, unexamined. I wondered whether Y. might have understood Greek—hardly any Germans did—but then decided the man in civilian clothes at the desk in Y's office probably had understood it. The sun, the sky, the streets looked wonderful to me, as I walked back to my office.

Dimitrios also was released shortly afterwards, although he did not get his food stamps back. Several of us helped him through the month by sharing food stamps and food itself. He continued working at the Robert Bosch company till the war ended, and then returned to Greece without further run-ins with the Gestapo.

Working at Bosch, I had learned to speak Greek as fluently as I now speak English, and was in demand all over the factory to help train the Greek DP's. Among the Greeks there were a very few who were somewhat educated, and among this very small number the best educated was Kharalambos Khazantsoglou (yes, I transliterate correctly! Greek names are real tongue twisters). I shall call him K. for short.

K. was a small dapper man in his early thirties. His eyes were of that luminous, piercing light grey which stands out in one's memory and which makes the person seem very cold and emotionless. His hair was prematurely grey, almost white. He would always dress in a light grey-blue suit, white shirt and grey-blue tie. His face had good, clear features which would have made him handsome except for his paleness. He could smile on occasion, showing a set of flawless white teeth. I cannot remember any mirth in his smile ever—only a cold, cautious politeness to which it was impossible to respond except in like politeness. I remember his small hands and feet, small even relative to his small stature, I think. From the very beginning of our acquaintance, I felt for him special compassion. He seemed so withdrawn into himself, so purposefully aloof from others; and one thus self-isolated cannot be happy, as I sensed even then. Also I could well imagine what it must be like to live in crowded barracks with people who do not share your interests, without books (to me this alone has always seemed a great privation), without privacy, without family, without relief from this kind of environment except to work in a factory. And K. was evidently neither used to nor suited for factory work. But his personality and manner forbade closer contact or a show of sympathy.

K. was assigned to work, but soon began to be almost constantly absent. His foreman signed a complaint. Copies of such complaints were given to our own personnel office and put in special files. Two consecutive complaints, amounting to several weeks' continued absence, would result in the absentee's being called to our office where my boss (a good man whom I respected wholeheartedly and for whom it was good to work) would admonish the person and inform him or her that any further complaint would be sent to the Gestapo and would be cause for imprisonment in a "Labor Education Camp." After seven weeks' continued absence our office received the second complaint about K., and he was summoned to our office.

But meanwhile rumors had reached me privately, and my boss officially, through the manager of the barracks where K. was housed, that K. had actually been absent from work with the express permission of the Gestapo. He was supposed to be in their pay and employed on their special errands while assigned to work at our factory only as a "cover." My boss (an anti-Nazi at heart who loathed the Gestapo and anyone connected with it) became quite angry at this news. He instantly got on the telephone and spoke to that curious official in our Bosch factory whose title was "Factory Protection Officer" (Werks-abwehrbeamter). It was the function of this official to be the liaison between our factory and the Gestapo, and my boss asked him to verify whether K. was indeed in their employ, or whether he had cleverly manufactured this fictitious employment in order to shirk work at the factory. Soon the news came back: the Protection Officer had talked to an official in the Gestapo who had absolutely denied K.'s story.

"All right," my boss said to me, "when K. comes here, have him wait in the outer office and keep him there. Tell me he is here, and I will call the Protection Officer who will in turn have the Gestapo pick K. up." The implication—K.'s being sent forthwith to a "Labor Education Camp"—was not stated, but I think was clearly in the minds of my boss and myself.

It was the most hateful business I had ever been given to do. On the one hand I could clearly see the relative justice, in this instance, of what was planned for K. Also I was very perplexed for a reason I did not tell my boss. Dimitrios had told me that the person who had denounced him to the Gestapo was K! Other Greeks I knew confirmed to me that K. was a Gestapo spy. Therefore I could not understand that the Gestapo official in liaison with our "Protection Officer" had denied that K. was employed by the Gestapo. What was going on? Who was lying? And if K. was after all a Gestapo spy—then would the horrible punishment about to befall him not serve him right?

Yet, how could I have any part in sending a human being to those camps? How could I myself serve as it were the Gestapo by decoying K. in our office till they could arrest him?

All this was troubling me when K. arrived, icily polite as always, neatly turned out as always, small, thin, and frail as always. I should add one further fact here I forgot to mention before. At an earlier time K. had come to our office with a physician's prescription he asked me to translate, and which stated, to my pity and disgust (I was 18 at the time, and my generation was not nearly as frank about sex as young people are today) that he had contracted syphilis. It went through my mind that in a concentration camp any medical treatment he might need would not be given. Would he even emerge alive from seven weeks' beating and starvation in those camps—even supposing his term would be only for seven weeks as customary with these DP's for absenteeism? As I said before, Dimitrios had been in the prime of health and vigor, but he came back from the camp utterly broken and cringing.

I asked K. to sit down and wait here in the outer office for a few minutes—my boss was busy right now; I would tell my boss that K. was here, and he would see him soon. But I knew my manner was not the usual, and K. instantly perceived this.

"What is the matter?" he asked. "What is wrong? There is something you know, and you are not telling me. What is it? Tell me."

What was I going to say? How could I lie? Perhaps by informing K. of what was planned against him I could save his life. Was it right to save his life if he were serving the enemy, if he were a traitor to his people? How could I myself have part in directly causing a human being, this human being looking at me and imploring me to help him, to be tortured and perhaps killed?

I made my choice, and told him the story of how the Gestapo had been contacted and its official had denied that K. was in their employment. "That is because the official to whom your man spoke is not the one under whom I work," said K. "I work for X (he named a name which did not register with me in my turmoil). Do not tell our boss I am here. Or else tell him I would not stay here and wait. I will go to my Gestapo boss, and he will straighten all this out. Thank you for giving me the information I needed to save myself."

"All right," I said, "but don't tell them I actually gave you the information, or it will be my neck next." He promised he would not, and hurriedly left.

I went and told my boss that K. had been there, but had not wished to wait and had left. My boss shrugged. "All right," he said, "we don't have to assist the Gestapo. Let them catch him—perhaps pick him up at the barracks—as best they can." I think he too was relieved our part in K.'s arrest had come to naught. I hoped the entire episode was behind me.

But it was not. The next day I was summoned to the office of the Protection Officer. He told me K. had gone to the Gestapo official for whom he worked and would be used by the Gestapo elsewhere rather than in our factory, "which is fine with us," he added, or some words to that effect, which conveyed to me his dislike of both K. and the Gestapo. Then he said that K. had reported to the Gestapo that I had warned him. "Now before you confirm or deny his story," the official said, "I want to warn you that in our employment, and in your employment, we are not supposed to have pity on the people with whom we deal, and we are not supposed to warn them. Now tell me—did you warn him or not?"

Thus prepared, I of course denied I had warned K! The official nodded and said he would so inform the Gestapo, and that this was probably the end of the story. "It's too bad we have to be harassed about people like that," he said. His attitude could not have been plainer. I then and always thought of him as "one of us," i.e. anti-Nazi.

After World War II was over, I heard of K.'s ultimate fate. He was placed on a train carrying Greeks back to Greece. During the trip, other Greeks recognized him as the Gestapo spy, beat him to death, and threw him off the train.

Death Comes Near

IN ALL the war, I never got as much as a scratch—with one exception.

We had had many air raid alerts before. I had never paid any attention. "There won't be any bombing," I would predict. "I won't go to the basement, Gertrud," I would tell the maid in the house who would knock at my door to urge me to get up and take shelter after the sirens sounded. "You'll see, nothing will happen." And I would turn over in bed and actually fall asleep again. I was cocksure about the whole thing! And I was right. No bombings nearby. I was also dead tired, for at that time I was working on my book manuscript.

So it was not till one night in 1944—it must have been summer, I am sure, I'll tell you why in a moment—that the sirens sounded, I awoke, and there was no feeling of safety in me. "Go get up. Get your emergency suitcase. Go down to the basement. Don't delay. Practice it. Get used to it." These warning thoughts surged up in me, too strong to ignore. I obeyed and went down to the basement, much to the surprise of the old lady, Mrs. Pistorius, who owned the house, her son-in-law Dr. Knoerzer, and Gertrud the maid. "It's going to be serious this time," I announced. And sure enough, for the first time in the war bombs fell. You could feel the ground shake a little, and we could hear the high whining sound of bombs falling, but not near us. Then the all-clear sounded, and we went back to our rooms. Through my window, which faced east, I could see a red light toward the north-east—fire where the bombs had hit.

I think it was two nights later that the sirens sounded again. This time there was no warning in my mind—because I knew I must get up and seek shelter, without warning. And this time it was terrifying. It's 33 years ago now *[1977]*, and the memory has dulled, but the fear reawakens a little as I think of the roar of the airplanes nosediving for the bombing, then the bombs whistling, and then the thuds as they hit. It went on for some time. Then there was quiet—no, not really, you could hear rubble settling, and the crackling of fire, and finally all clear sirens far away, not our own one close by.

We went to the basement exit. We could not open the door! It was blocked by crushed cement, plaster, and wood. We—myself and Gertrud, both of us young—pushed. Mrs. Pistorius was in her eighties and in great grief, for we all knew our house, this house in which Mrs. Pistorius had lived most of her life and raised her family, was almost totally destroyed. She remained seated in the basement. Gertrud and I pushed and pushed against that door till finally we had it open wide enough to get through.

We gasped! Normally we would have stood in the main hallway of the house, all enclosed. Instead, we stood on a pile of crumbling rubble from which smoke still went up—not smoke of fire, but plaster dust. One side of the house was sheared off entirely. The stairs leading to the second floor were there, but in the open. My room was still there—with one wall gone, the roof gone—but my bed, my wardrobe, all that was mine still there although covered with rocks and glass splinters from the shattered windows. Our street was impassable!

Not far off flames were roaring sky high, illuminating the entire chaotic scene. A huge tree which had been in Mrs. Pistorius' back yard was totally uprooted, and on its roots, upright, standing in what had been her bedroom. Across the street, we now saw, was a gaping hole where the house of the neighbors across the street had been. The hole was a crater, really. It was where the bomb falling nearest us had hit. We never did find out what became of those neighbors; they were almost certainly killed in that air raid. Our house had been destroyed by the concussion of that bomb as it fell.

I climbed upstairs on those open stairs to see what I might salvage from my room. Gertrud warned me that the stairs might collapse; I said I would risk it, and made my way to what had been my room. It was uncanny—I found that every single bit of property I owned in that room was there, reachable—not a single thing lost! By the light of the fires nearby, and in the warm air (that's how I know it must have been summer), I rummaged around, clearing off plaster and dust, packing clothes and books into my two big suitcases. I went to the washstand to get my toothbrush. The washstand was covered with huge glass splinters from the nearby window (there was no more windowpane, only broken fragments of the window frame). I stretched out my right hand too quickly—and stared at my index finger. A big flap of skin and tissue was nearly cut off from the top of its middle segment, no doubt by glass, and the blood gushed down my hand. It didn't even hurt much right then; I stared at my finger as though it were someone else's. All I had to fix it was a handkerchief, which I tied around my finger, pressing the loose tissue and skin in its place as tightly as I could. I think the handkerchief was soon soaked with blood, but what could I do about it? Nothing, that's what—and besides, I was too busy, and this night was far too exciting.

That was it—the only scratch I ever received in all of World War II or all the 12 years of the Nazis. I wouldn't have received it but for my own hastiness. As you know, it has healed absolutely perfectly—for years now I haven't even been able to distinguish the fine white scar that used to outline the healed-back patch of skin.

Another room was preserved for us—the bathroom! Just what we needed, though of course there was no running water. But the bathtub had been kept full to the brim for emergencies. For three days we subsisted on water from that bathtub for washing (face and fingers), cooking, drinking. "We" were Mrs. Pistorius, Gertrud, Dr. Knoerzer and his family of 5 (I think—it may have been more), and I.

We rescued a little grill from somewhere—the kitchen was gone, so I don't know how we found it, perhaps from the basement—we cooked in tin cans and one pan, over a fire made from wood out of the rubble, and even had hot tea, and on one festive occasion, a big fish. At night, of course, we were in the basement. Then finally we went our separate ways.

Mrs. Pistorius rented a room in a midtown apartment building. About three weeks later it was totally destroyed, with everyone living there. I don't know what became of Gertrud—I seem to remember she moved away from Stuttgart and survived the war. I did not mind separating from her, as I had wondered whether she might not have been spying on me for the Gestapo. The Knoerzers all survived the war, and so did their house, that is, it was damaged, but could be repaired, and was after the war. Dr. Knoerzer was the head of the Finance Department at Robert Bosch. I still exchange Christmas letters with him.

I moved into a home for female employees of the Bosch Company, not too far from the Pistorius house. It was near a gigantic air raid shelter built into the side of one of the hills surrounding the city. It was one of the safest shelters anywhere—in it, you couldn't even hear the bombs falling, nor feel the thud of the ground when bombs hit. In the late weeks of the war, we would go there late in the evening, sleep there, and go to work directly from there the next morning. At that time I had my book manuscript finished, so it must have been late summer. Actually, where to keep the manuscript was a problem! I think, though I am not sure any more, that finally I brought it home to the farm and left it there at Christmas 1944.

You cannot imagine how it is when a whole country breaks down completely. To me, witnessing this of the hated Nazi Germany was like strong wine—exciting, adventurous, longed for, finally happening. I savored it all with the thoughtlessness and cruelty of one who has no dependents.

It was now April 1945, and for months—ever since the fall of 1944—we could hear the rumbling of cannon fire to the west. For months, American bomber planes had hit Stuttgart almost daily without resistance. Now the end was in sight, could arrive almost any moment. I still had to be cautious, but it was easy now—"only a few more weeks at most, and you'll be crushed," I inwardly called to the Nazis and most Germans. We spent more time in the air raid shelters than at work. The inner city was a rubble heap, with the stench of smoldering fire, and decaying bodies deep under the broken girders, bricks and rubble. Transportation kept breaking down, telephones usually did not work, nothing except food could be bought, records and files were gone, our work at the office was a sham. We non-Nazis (and in my office everyone was a non-Nazi except one of the Displaced Persons camp leaders, a Mr. Fritz Hermann) exchanged news of the German retreats and defeats with equanimity. Soon this insanity would end. It wasn't possible that it could last much longer.

In this mood, Easter of 1945 approached, and with it a small vacation. I caught the train from Stuttgart to the town nearest our farm on the rail line. It was packed. Every 15 minutes or so it would stop because of enemy airplanes strafing us from overhead. Finally, late in the evening, it got to Heilbronn, some 25 kilometers from our farm. "This is the end of the line," an official announced. "The rails have been bombed ahead of us, and cannot be repaired. Everybody out."

So everybody got out. We started walking along the main highway. There was a brilliant moon overhead, so brilliant it was not really dark. You could hear the droning of airplanes—"Ami" planes of course; there hadn't been German planes for many, many weeks. You could hear the ever-present and much closer cannon rumble. Behind us the sky was a fiery red where Heilbronn and other towns further south had been bombed and were burning. It would take three to four hours to walk to the farm, if there were no detours and no delays caused by traffic hazards and bombings. Conceivably, we could be killed.

This might be our last night alive. You could sense this realization sink in. Those of us who were walking were the young and physically fit. Older people stayed behind in Heilbronn, or rested by the wayside till daybreak. But we went on. Among us were German soldiers, foreign workers, men and women. There wasn't much talking. Even yet, the specter of the Gestapo was with us. Even yet, one incautious remark might get you shot down on the spot. No, better not to talk.

And then here and there a man and a woman would draw together, walk hand in hand, or his arm around her waist or her shoulders. They had been strangers before, now they were close—for this night might be all they had left.

A young man sidled up to me. A few broken words in German, and I knew he was a Serbian (from Yugoslavia). We could converse by his speaking Serbian very slowly, and I speaking Russian very slowly. His face was pale, unshaven, hazy, unreal in the moonlight.

Pretty soon this man wanted to hold hands with me. For a while I let him. Then I withdrew my hand. For there, just a few steps from us, right by the roadside, one of the other couples was copulating in full view of all. Some of the passers-by chuckled. Others turned their heads. Yet others—pulled off the road themselves.

I walked much faster, separating from the Serbian, separating from the whole pack of people. If that is how they wished to spend this night, possibly their last in life—for airplanes were approaching again, and they did rake the ground with shots, flying very low—then all right, that was their choice. But not mine. I shook my head and looked straight ahead. Not this. No, not this. Not this chaotic, meaningless throwing myself away. No, not even if I would never "be with a man" in my life. No, never like this. Only with real love.

This decision, too, I count as our Lord's grace and blessing. I made it home, totally unharmed, the next morning. Mine had been perhaps the last train out of Stuttgart that made it even to Heilbronn.

Things often looked so desperately black for my family in Germany under the Nazis. We lived right in the "belly of the beast," so to speak, and my mother was Jewish! All through the Nazi years, of course, the intimidation, vilification and persecution of the Jewish people continued and intensified. I well remember the signs in stores and restaurants saying "Jews not welcome here" and at the entrances of many towns, "This town is 'judenrein' (cleansed of Jews)."

The time came when Jews had to wear large yellow stars on all their outer clothing; however, my mother, along with other Jews married to "Aryans," was exempt from this requirement. She did have to carry her Jewish I.D. card at all times, and I think later on she could have been arrested (which meant probable torture and even death) for using public transportation, or eating in a restaurant (which had been one of her favorite pleasures). She did do both all through the Nazi period, though, I suppose, always in fear. This constant fear and tension must have accounted in part for her frequent outbursts of temper, which I hated more and more.

The last trial of my father's faith under the Nazis came in May 1945. Just as World War II was ending in Germany, in the very last days of actual fighting, a unit of the dreaded Nazi SS troops came to my parents' farm, located on a hill, to make a "last stand" there against the approaching American troops. The SS ordered our family and farm workers to leave. We walked away from there behind a horse-drawn wagon loaded with the few necessities we had already packed in advance for this kind of eventuality. We slowly walked toward the wood east of the farm. I remember thinking we might see our home destroyed within the next few minutes, together with all the valuables there, in particular some beautiful porcelain heirlooms.

For a while nothing happened. Then, after about half an hour, we saw the SS remove their machine guns from our garden and drive off. We turned our horses and wagon around and walked back to the farm. Nothing was hurt at all, not one window was shattered, even the garden and the fields remained reasonably undisturbed.

My dear father's trust in God was vindicated again. Father's oft repeated saying, "You must have trust in God' ("Ihr muesst Gottvertrauen haben!") held true. Ever since that day, earthly treasures, like our lovely porcelain, have meant relatively little to me. War teaches us that earthly ownership is a very fragile thing.

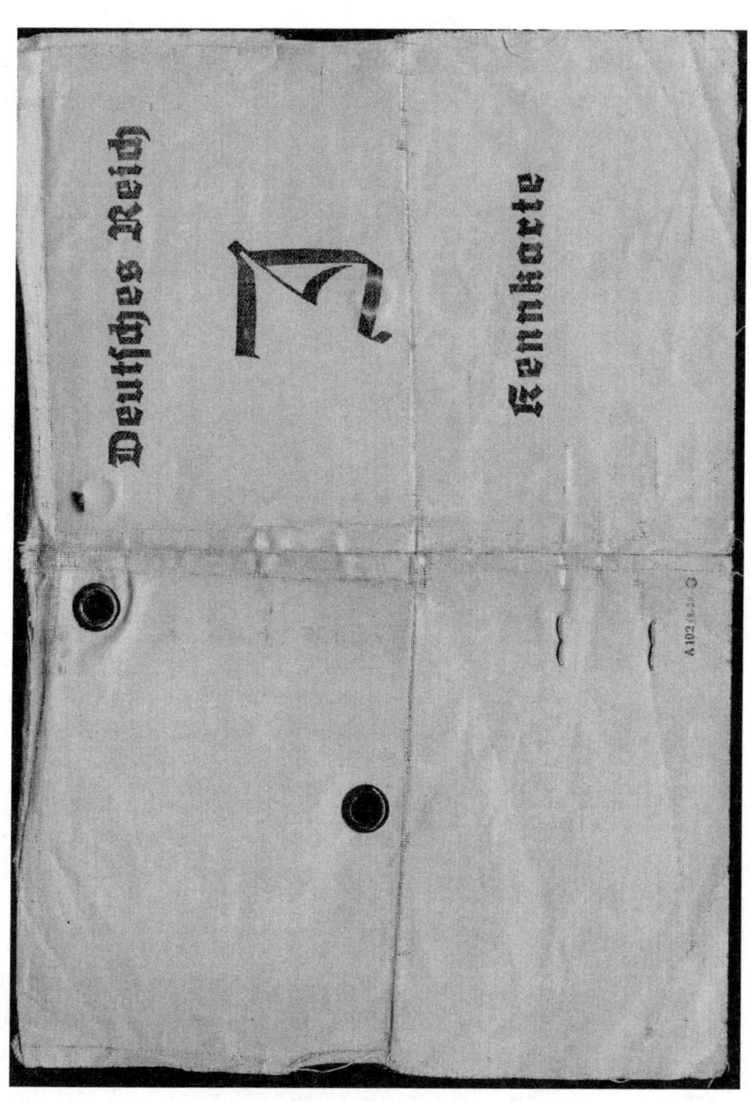

My mother's Jewish ID, outside view.

Kennort:	
Kennnummer:	
Gültig bis	1944
Name	
Vornamen	
Geburtstag	
Geburtsort	
Beruf	
Unveränderliche Kennzeichen	Keine
Veränderliche Kennzeichen	Keine
Bemerkungen:	Keine

(Unterschrift des Kennkarteninhabers)

, den 24. 1939

(Ausfertigende Behörde)

Polizeipräsident in Berlin

(Unterschrift des ausfertigenden Beamten)

Linker Zeigefinger

Rechter Zeigefinger

My mother's Jewish ID, inside view.

Leaving

AFTER World War II ended in May 1945, I spent several weeks at home. During this time my cousin, Carl Cremer from Chicago, visited us. He was the son of my father's younger brother, "Uncle Fritz" (Frederick) Cremer. Uncle Fritz had married a Jewish American lady, "Aunt Joe" (Josephine) Italie. They had one child, my cousin Carl (also known among us as "Carl Cremer III"). When he came to see us, Carl was 31 and a good six feet tall, handsome with dark hair and eyes like his mother. He was a Major in the American Army. He was able to bring us American food and clothes that his parents sent to him for us. We appreciated this very much.

Mother, Father, and I dining at the farm.

During those several weeks at home I was exposed again to my mother's temper explosions. I felt I could not stand them any longer, so I determined to run away from home and return to Stuttgart. I think it was June 18, 1945, but it could have been a day or two before or after, that I "ran away." Life with my mother had become intolerable to me. It seemed there was a screaming, explosive, degrading tantrum almost every day, which the evening contrition and excuses and in-between tenderness could not outweigh. It had been bad enough formerly during vacations, with the return to Stuttgart promising relief. Now, with no sure escape on the horizon, I could not stand it any more. My dear patient friend, Laura, was with us then. I watched her and my father patiently bear my mother's rages and moods, listen to her outbursts, her swearing by the hour. "Not for me," I thought. "Laura can leave, and my father is married to Mother, but I will not go on like this. I will somehow get back to Stuttgart as soon as possible, when the French no longer occupy it. I will go back to work for Robert Bosch, or perhaps for the American Military government."

But how to leave? How to get there?

The opportunity came when the mayor of Allfeld, the small village nearest the farm, needed to go to the county seat, Mosbach, to have a conference with the American military government there, and needed me to come along as his interpreter. This meant my leaving on a bicycle and bicycling with the mayor to Mosbach, about an hour away by bicycle; then staying there for the conference, and then returning. This would require my absence from home for some three to five hours without being missed. With luck, I would return early, bicycle past the cutoff from the main road to our farm, and go on towards Stuttgart. With extra luck, someone might give me a ride.

I could not take much with me, because it would have aroused suspicion. A change of clothes, an extra pair of shoes, hardly anything at all, only what could be stuffed tightly into my biggest purse. Thank goodness, it was summer, so no need yet to worry about winter clothes.

I did not dare tell even my friend Laura, nor my father, about what I had in mind. I think perhaps they were not too surprised later, because I did toss out the threat, "One of these days I may just get back to Stuttgart somehow." Another threat, given later, and shortly before I actually did leave, and then deliberately to lead them astray, was that I might try to get to Heidelberg (north of our farm, instead of south toward Stuttgart) and matriculate at the university there.

Heidelberg had the advantage of being situated on the same road as Mosbach, so I could have just gone on from there after the conference with the mayor. I do not recall this exactly now, but it seems to me I may have separated from him in Mosbach, telling him I wanted to do some shopping before returning. But I may just have gone back with him to Allfeld, where he stopped, and from where I continued. In any case, we were through in Mosbach in record time.

The hardest moment was when I actually pedaled my bicycle past the cutoff to our farm. Up to that moment, it seemed that I could still reconsider. Up to that moment, I really had not made a hard and fast decision. But when I left that little road wending its way up the hill to our farm behind; I hardened. I hardened to the point where there was no regret, only a joyous grimness, or grim joy, and with it all an expectation of newness of life, adventure. Nor did I doubt at all that all would go well! I look back today, and it seems incredible that I could have been so totally confident.

I bicycled on for a good hour and reached Heilbronn, the next large city. It had been largely leveled by the air raids, but some cleanup work had been done, and the main streets were passable.

And there, in Heilbronn, was a huge, open truck parked by the side of the street. It seemed that for ten Marks—a ridiculously low sum!—the truck driver would take as many people and their bicycles, if any, with him to Stuttgart—no in-between stops. "We'll get there well before curfew this afternoon," he said. I was one of the 30 or so people who got there in time to get a ride. And so, with no breakdown of any kind, we found ourselves in Stuttgart late that afternoon, as he had said. *He* made 300 Marks. *We* were jubilant.

Not only that, but I was able to make friends with another girl on that truck. When I explained my situation to her—that I was returning to Stuttgart where I had worked during the war, and hoped to find work again, but had no place to stay—she invited me to stay at her place, and I was all fixed up. Yes, my expectancy of things turning out well was fulfilled. Then I called it luck when I gave it more than fleeting thought. Today I praise our Lord for all His love and care.

The very next morning I applied for a job with the US Military Government in Stuttgart. I was told to check back later as to whether I had gotten a job or not. As I walked out of the building, I noticed a couple of Russian officers. I approached them and asked in Russian whether they might need someone to work for them. "Why, of course," they said. "Come right along with us to our headquarters. We are with the Soviet liaison office here in Stuttgart." They had a car there, and took me with them on the spot.

I came with them to their building in Bad Cannstatt (a nice Stuttgart suburb). Here I met a Russian girl officer, Valya, and "the commissar"—Licutenant Boris Shpak, a dark stocky man with somewhat Mongol features. The officers who had picked me up were Lieutenant Danilov, a tall handsome blond fellow of perhaps 26, and Lieutenant Vassily (I can't remember his last name), tall, thin, pale, long upturned nose, and high-pitched voice. Later I learned from Valya that Vassily was the *real* Communist commissar—Shpak was this supposedly, but Vassily had the real power. This was confirmed several weeks later when Vassily, not Shpak, was involved in trying to kidnap a young Volga German girl and her mother to force them back to Soviet Russia—but I am getting ahead of my story.

Soon after my arrival, I was invited to have dinner with them. You should have seen the dinner—a table groaning with food, namely, American food, especially the snowy white bread, butter, canned corned beef, coffee, I forget what else, but there was more than plenty, including hard drinks. I never have liked these, and sat back to watch as the Russians got drunker and drunker, encouraging each other to drink more, yelling "bottoms-upski!" and becoming more and more boisterous. Valya began playing the piano—the building they lived in must have been some wealthy German residence—and Lt. Danilov began to dance Russian dances including the kind where you crouch and kick your legs forward. He was a tall man with long legs, and it seemed impossible that he should be good at this kind of dance, but surprisingly he was—he was excellent.

Finally it all stopped, and they said of course I was to stay with them at their house—and Valya took me upstairs to palatial bedrooms, one of which she shared with me. She locked us in—I was so stupid that until she told me I had not even thought there might be a need for this—and then we visited. Valya was a good girl, about my age or a little older (I had just turned 20) and I think if we met again, we would recognize one another and immediately go on from where we stopped then—we liked each other and had confidence in one another. We slept well and without interruptions—and the next morning there was more eating, and no work at all. "Later, later," I was told when asking what I was to do, "just eat, enjoy yourself, talk to Valya."

After lunch—another big meal—Boris Shpak asked me whether I would like some nylon stockings. "We have plenty of them down in the basement," he said. "Just come with me and look them over and choose which ones you want."

You may think I was crazy, but I unsuspectingly went down to the basement with him. Indeed there was all kinds of clothing, shipped in by the Americans for the Russian allies, I suppose, for it was al American. Shpak escorted me into the room, then locked the doo behind us and removed the key from the lock. That is when it dawned on me what he wanted with me. He approached and I could smell the liquor on his breath.

Strangely, I was not really afraid, nor angry—the poor man was half drunk and probably lonely—and besides, at that time Russians and Communists were still heroes and rescuers from the Nazis for me. "If you had a sister, you would not like to have this happen to her," I told him. He nodded, and I think we kissed each other. Then he wordlessly pulled out the key and unlocked the door, and even stuffed several pairs of nylon stockings into my jacket pocket. Then we climbed the stairs back up to the first floor again. Valya looked at me strangely, then smiled—she could see all was well.

But I wanted no repetitions of such a scene. So I simply walked out of the house, and back to Stuttgart proper, about 45 minutes' walk. I returned to the American Military Government office and asked whether I had got the job I had applied for—and lo and behold, I had! I was to work as an interpreter-secretary in the Displaced Persons' Office, for Lieutenant Robert E. Coulehan, a young man just a year older than I. We got along splendidly from the very first. This job with Lt. Coulehan was the *last* opening at the US Military Government—and I would not have gotten it, had I applied even *one day* later. (Lt. Coulehan told me that himself later.)

Oh yes, I forgot to tell you one incident that happened right after I arrived at the Russian residence in Bad Cannstatt, and before they invited me to dinner. Their friendliness was really not all that miraculous as it may have appeared. For when I first arrived there, another Russian was visiting there—and when he saw me, he rushed toward me, hugged me and kissed me and exclaimed, "Lenochka, Lenochka, you saved my life! This is the German girl who worked at Robert Bosch who saved my life!"

And indeed it appeared I had. He was another Communist commissar. I can see him as I remember this—tall, black hair, good build, sparkling dark eyes, very good-looking even though with smallpox marks. He had been a "displaced person" foreign worker in the Robert Bosch factory where I had worked as interpreter-secretary during the War. The Gestapo had inquired about him, searching for him as a "commissar." Had they gotten to him they would have killed him. I "lost" his file, as I "lost" several others, because his name was not spelled correctly in the German transliteration of the Russian sounds. I knew he was the person they were looking for, but said no person by the name *they* gave was employed by Robert Bosch–so the Gestapo never did find him.

Well, when he told Danilov, Shpak and the rest of them this story, of course I was "in" with them. Maybe that is why nothing harmful happened to me. And why would he be there at the precise moment when I arrived? Then, I called it lucky coincidence. Today, I joy in our Lord, Who times our steps perfectly.

The Villa Reizenstein

Perfect Timing

SOMETIMES I think that if I had not walked down a certain flight of stairs in the Villa Reizenstein in Stuttgart, Germany, in one certain, exact moment of time, I would never have met my husband. And my wonderful children, grandchildren, and great-grandchildren would not be here.

It was shortly before Christmas in December, 1945, while I was still working for the local American Military Government under Lt. Coulehan in Stuttgart. My father had sent me with a personal letter from him to an old friend, Mr. Erich Rossmann, a former delegate to the "Reichstag," or German Parliament. Rossmann was now the "Laenderratssekretaer" (that's a *short* German combination word!), or secretary to the "Laenderrat." The Laenderrat was the council of the German "Lands" (states/provinces) of the zone of Germany then administered by the U.S.A. I used my lunch time to deliver the letter.

The "Laenderrat" and its corresponding U.S. Military Government office, the "Regional Government Coordinating Office" (RGCO), were located in the Villa Reitzenstein. The Villa was a sumptuous edifice on the top of one of the hills surrounding Stuttgart, built around 1900 by a Baron Reizenstein. I had heard of it, but never been inside it.

I made my way to the Villa, found the office of Mr. Rossmann on the second floor and delivered my father's letter. The building was totally unaffected by the wartime destruction, and sumptuous inside and out. After leaving Mr. Rossmann's office, I walked back down the wide marble stairs coverd by thick red carpeting. I walked very slowly so I could take in the sight of this imposing hall with its marble columns, the grand piano, the many wall mirrors with gilded frames, all of it fit for the reception of kings and heads of state. As I was walking down, up the stairs came a man wearing the uniform and shoulder insignia of an American army major. I myself was wearing a lovely black coat with fur collar, nylon hose and nice shoes from America. We met halfway.

"Are you looking for someone?" he asked, observing my looking all about, and slowness. "Perhaps I can help you." He spoke in English, obviously assuming or expecting that I would understand.

I made a quick decision.

"Yes, I am looking for Dr. James Pollock," I replied.

Now here is what made me say this: Lt. Coulehan, my boss in the local Military Displaced Persons' office (which was about to be disbanded) had told me of Dr. Pollock, the Senior Advisor to General Eisenhower's successor as European Theater Commander in the RGCO, General Lucius Clay. Lt. Coulehan had suggested that I ought to apply for a job with him. The job would consist of translating aloud, sentence by sentence, General Clay's official public speeches to the assembled Minister Presidents of the German Laender (comparable to state governors here in America), and interpreting at his private meetings with them, as well as at other American-German government conferences.

I had not followed up on Lt. Coulehan's suggestion, because at that time I had two other job possibilities. One was to return to the Robert Bosch Company, from which I was officially "on leave." The other was with a German book publisher to whom I had offered a novel I was then working on (not the one mentioned before, which was already in process of publication). The job with the publishing company needed only my signature on their contract to make this commitment final. This is what makes my quick decision to ask for Dr. Pollock all the more surprising—and at that very moment I even wondered, "Now, what made me say that?"

"I am Major Kane, and I am Dr. Pollock's deputy," said the major. "You can see him right now." (Remember, this was the lunch hour). "What do you wish to see him about?"

"I understand he may be looking for an interpreter," I said.

"Yes, he is. Come with me right now," said Major Kane. Dumbfounded, I walked downstairs with him and was ushered into a beautiful wood-paneled office, which was furnished in keeping with the wealth and elegance of the rest of the building. I was introduced to a tall, bald, slightly portly American with rimless spectacles, wearing a military uniform with "civilian" insignia, sitting behind a huge desk. Major Kane explained that I had come to ask for a job as interpreter.

Dr. James Pollock, senior advisor to Gen. Lucius Clay.

"Wonderful," said Dr. Pollock. "We are looking for an interpreter for General Clay himself. What is your name?"

"Ellen Cremer."

"Cremer? How do you spell it?"

I spelled it.

"Are you by any chance related to a Dr. Carl Cremer who was a deputy in the German Parliament before 1933?"

Hardly believing the question, I explained that Dr. Cremer was my father.

"I met your father when I was on a study tour of Germany with a group of American Political Science students. He was the German official guiding us around the Reichstag (Parliament building)," Dr. Pollock explained happily, smiling broadly and obviously welcoming me. "You won't have any trouble with 'de-nazification' then! All we'll have to do is see whether you will be able to translate speeches sentence by sentence. Let me just try it now."

He pulled a sheaf of papers from a stack of documents and read a sentence. "Now translate this into German," he said. I proceeded. It did not seem very hard—all I had to do was concentrate. He gave me a few more sentences from General Clay's previous speeches to translate, nodding happily as I translated fluently and without mistakes.

"All right," he said. "You're hired! We'll settle your salary and so on later—Major Kane, you see to that, and that all the papers are filled in. We'll see you here on January 2, 1946 at 9 A.M."

I walked out of that building in a complete daze. The interview had only taken about fifteen minutes. I had my Christmas vacation—about ten days—to think it over. But really I had made up my mind—or it was made up for me—right then in Dr. Pollock's office.

From this "chance" encounter followed two and a half years as General Clay's interpreter, a most challenging, exciting, instructive job, which also entailed high wages and much publicity in German newspapers. I was famous! From this encounter also followed my meeting my future husband, Kenneth L. Myers, who was on General Clay's staff. From this followed my marriage, my coming to the United States, and the lives of all my children and grandchildren.

So, if I had not walked down those stairs in that precise moment Major Kane was walking upstairs—if I had not dawdled longer than usual—and then, if I had not immediately asked to see Dr. Pollock—I would not be sitting here tonight—I would not have met my husband—my whole life would have been much different.

Dr. Pollock's sharp memory for people and names helped, too!

A light moment with General Clay as I interpret.

The photo from my German ID card issued February 2, 1946.

Interpreting at the publication of the Denazification Law of March 5, 1946.

General Clay signed this photo for me a month later at a subsequent speech before the Council of Minister Presidents (Laenderrat) in Stuttgart. When I asked him for his signature, he was ready to leave, but waited patiently until I brought him this photo and a pen.

Interpreting for Mr. Von Dorrer of the Laenderrat Secretariat
on September 10, 1946.

Top: Interpreting at a live radio address given by U.S. Secretary of Agriculture Clinton P. Anderson on July 5, 1947. Averell Harriman is seated on the right. Bottom: Listening intently at an interpreting session in 1947.

A press photo from 1946. I was very proud of this picture because the photographer was famous throughout Europe, and she had taken a picture of me *and* signed it! I felt that this proved how very important I was. Now I know that I was just very conceited.

Please untie me! Knots
sometimes hide things.

3 March 1948

Dearest Ellen:
a small token of my
esteem for the third finger
of your left hand.
Kenneth

Stuttgart, Germany

The notes with the bouquet, March 3, 1948

My engagement ring was hidden in a knot among the ribbons with the flowers Ken gave me that morning. He simply dropped off a bouquet with my landlady and drove away, while my landlady(!) carried the flowers to me.
The evening before, at a costume party, Ken—dressed as Aunt Jemima—had said something about our "marriage papers."
The upper note reads, "Please untie me! Knots sometimes hide things."

Ken

I FIRST met my dear husband, Kenneth L. Myers, October 28, 1946. He was Economics Officer of the "Land" (state/province) of Wuerttemberg-Baden. Ken was with the U.S. Military Government, then known in the American occupation alphabet soup as OMGUS. He came to the office where I worked at the Villa Reizenstein, together with another American civilian official, a Mr. Felix Stetson, to confer with some German officials about leather production in Wuerttemberg-Baden. I interpreted for him.

It was a Monday, and I must say Ken seemed awfully tired! "Big weekend behind you, mister," I thought. Because I had to write a report of such meetings, I am able to pin down the date of our first meeting exactly.

Ken escorts me to interpret at an OMGUS conference, December 3, 1946—the second time we met.

The next time we met was December 3, 1946. General Hugh B. Hester, the chief of the Agriculture Division of OMGUS from Berlin, and just one step below General Clay, came for a conference and public address. (General Hester was later exposed publicly as a Communist! You could have knocked me down with a feather when I heard of it years later. He actually defected to Czechoslovakia in about 1950, I believe.) Because I was General Clay's official interpreter, and therefore known as the "best," I was loaned by my office to OMGUS Wuerttenberg-Baden to translate for General Hester. And Ken was the one to arrange this, pick me up, escort me around, and bring me back.

It was as we walked up the stairs of the big government building to the conference room where General Hester was to speak that I suddenly thought, "This man is going to be my husband." At that very moment some German photographer took a picture of us walking side by side. We were both smiling. I received a copy of that picture.

It was not till January 1947 that Ken called and we had our first date. From there on out we became closer and closer. I put the picture of Ken and I into a little book I made for Ken's next birthday, November 23, 1947, in which I told the story of our growing closeness. Three months after this, on March 3, 1948, we were engaged to be married.

I enjoyed many activities with Ken during our courtship and engagement, including fishing and hunting.

Ken was interested and knowledgeable in so many areas! This was very important to me. Music, art, history, politics, economics, philosophy, education, books we had read, people we both knew—we had so much to share. Had he been younger, I wonder if the feedback would have been as rich and thorough. How wonderful to have someone who was not bored by classical music and encouraged me to practice and play, though Ken's *preference* ran more to "Lawrence Welk"-type music. How great to see someone choose good art, patronize young German artists, exhibit good taste!

Another photo of me with Ken as escort.

I finally had found someone I did not think I would ever *outgrow*, someone not awed by what I knew, someone *happy* with my thirst for reading, someone who would not stifle me. He might not echo my exact preferences—but he would not stop me, nor feel threatened by all these interests in me, because he, too, thought them good.

Ken loved children and wanted many of them. This, too, was a *must* in my choice of a husband. Ken would give parties for German children—once thirty or more of them from all over the neighborhood. He also wanted a wife who would "be a joyful mother of children (Psalm 113)." This was very deep in him because of his own very unhappy childhood.

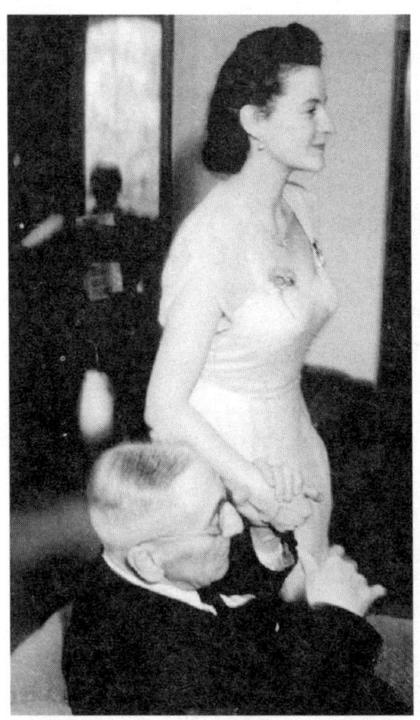

Left: My father holds my hand at my wedding.
Right: Ken and I on our wedding day, July 2, 1948.

What really made me love him, however, was the depth of his own sympathy for others, especially those wronged. One of the decisive moments in our relationship was one occasion—it must have been the spring or early summer of 1947—when he gave a speech to some gathering. In the speech he mentioned the Polish officers whom he had met during his service in the army, and who could not return to their homeland because if they did they would be killed by the Communists. As he spoke of them, expatriated in England now after World War II, tears came to his eyes and started streaming down his face, and finally he had to stop speaking. This is when my heart went out to him. This is what I wanted most deeply of all—a heart that could be touched, really touched, with the trouble of others, or over a true cause. I did not want a talker, but a true man. And so I have always found him. And so, I pray, I shall always find my dear sons.

Sooner or later every young couple in love and contemplating marriage chooses their own special song they think of as "our song." At the time Ken and I began dating, the song below was very popular, and eventually we thought of it as "our song":

YOU BELONG TO MY HEART (1943)

Words by Ray Gilbert © Ipanema Music Used by permission

You belong to my heart
Now and forever,
And our love had its start
Not long ago;
We were gathering stars
While a million guitars
Played our love song.
When I said, "I love you,"
Every beat of my heart said it too!

'Twas a moment like this,
Do you remember?
And your eyes threw a kiss,
When they met mine;
Now we own all the stars
And the million guitars
Are still playing;
Darling, you are the song,
And you'll always belong to my heart!

Ken, my father, and I at our wedding reception.

The photo from my last German ID card, issued July 13, 1948 to Ellen *Myers*.
Just a month later, Ken and I were in New York.

With Ken's Family

KEN'S dad, Attorney Edwin F. Myers, or "Pa," first wrote me in 1948 after Ken and I became engaged. It was a friendly letter, and like almost all his correspondence and conversation it was filled with conservative political remarks. Pa was fiercely conservative! Among his four sons (there were no daughters), Ken was the most in agreement with him.

Ken did not mind my atheism/agnosticism and did not protest when I refused to be married in a church. Ken had grown up in Nebraska and belonged to a Protestant mainline church. When he was nine years old, he had obeyed an altar call to receive Christ as his Savior in that church's summer youth camp. But later, when attending Harvard University, he came to believe that Christianity was not the only, but merely the best, way to God and for life. So we were married at the German "Standesamt" (civil marriage registrar) in Stuttgart on July 2, 1948, and arrived in New York on August 14.

We visited my mother's older brother, Leon, and his wife in Washington, D.C. and my father's brother, Fritz, and his family (who had sent my family American clothing through their son, Carl, in 1945) in Chicago. Then we made our way to my husband's hometown, Broken Bow, Nebraska, where we stayed for about 18 months with my parents-in-law.

Our first child, Kenneth L. Myers, Jr., was born there. Upon this joyful event I received a letter from my father, which read in part:

> It is now 40 years ago that I entrusted my life to God's guidance. I have never regretted it! Our Lord blessed me with a good wife and daughter. True, the Nazi time! But He saw us safely through it. I wish you could come to Him, too, but everyone must take this step for himself.

I kept the letter in our baby scrapbook for little Kenny, but it meant little to me until eleven years later.

We attended the local mainline Protestant church in which my husband had been brought up. I was instantly received as a new member. No one asked me what I believed (I was as atheist/agnostic as ever). I was a member of the locally prominent Myers family, and that was sufficient. No one spoke of God or spiritual things. Attendance was useful for business contacts. I never heard of any private Bible study. I was in the choir; the anthems and hymns containing Scripture were the only signposts to Christ, and those were overlooked. I enjoyed the monthly potluck dinners. In the home no prayers were offered, nor did I miss them. Having exhausted the small local library, and starving for serious reading, I looked into my mother-in-law's books by Agnes Sanford, a forerunner of today's 'New Age' thought, but by God's unacknowledged merciful protection I did not warm to them.

Ken's mother, Christie Julie Haumont Myers, or "Gammy" to you children, was an excellent cook and seamstress. She operated her own interior decorating business, the "Christie Shoppe", on the second floor of Pa's "Myers Building" in downtown Broken Bow. Unfortunately she ran it at a loss practically all the time, one of the causes of discord between her and Pa, who furiously paid her debts over and over again. She didn't give it up until after Pa's death.

Pa and Gammy's marriage was very unhappy from all I heard and all I could observe while Ken and I lived at the Myers residence from August 1948 to December 1949. Gammy once told me that before her marriage she had never been taught how children were born and somehow got the idea they came out of the mother by way of the navel! Thus she was not only in pain but terrified when her first baby was born–it wasn't moving in the right direction!

Gammy and Pa had four sons, and lost at least three children to miscarriages. Their oldest oldest son, Edwin, took to drinking early in life, dropped out of Harvard, entered the army in World War II, met and married a young war widow, Billie, in 1942 or '43. She had one daughter from her first marriage. They moved in with Pa in Broken Bow at the end of World War II. He was more or less drunk much of the time. After his wife, Billie, died and her daughter got married, he resided at Pa and Gammy's home or in Pa's office. One night while he was in a drunken state, the office caught fire from his carelessly placed smouldering cigarette. He died of asphyxiation in the fire.

Ken was the second son; he was in character much like Pa, and Gammy liked him the least. It was a very unhappy home. Gammy wanted a little girl very much, but when she didn't get one, she made up for it by dressing the two youngest boys (Frankie and Johnny) in girls' clothes, with girls' hairdos while they were little. When these boys were grown, Frank always remained his mother's boy, never becoming independent. Finally, he died most tragically along with Gammy and an elderly aunt.

John also never married and had psychiatric problems much of his short life; one of them was his infatuation with his mother. He graduated from college (University of California?) with a degree in phychology. He was a Christian of Pentecostal persuasion. He would go on prolonged fasts. On occasion he would do the most odd things, led, he believed, by God. For example, once he knelt down at the feet of an elderly black man on a main street in Wichita in broad daylight in front of many people, hugged the man's feet and asked his forgiveness. The man was very embarrassed. At other occasons he would tell people (once myself) that if they would just do this or that (in my case, touch the doorjamb), they would be healed of illnesses they didn't know they had. Yet John meant no harm. He worked conscientiously at the jobs he had, and zealously read his Bible every day. Eventually when he was fasting in Kansas City, he had a sunstroke, was taken to the hospital there and died in a coma, still in his 30s.

When I met the family, I liked Pa, whom I called "Father", which he liked very much—they had been calling him "Sire" before! Pa was a rough man showing little affection, which caused an emptiness in Gammy. His rougher homestead farm background clashed with her more refined European one. They shared no interests other than the material aspects of earning a living. Pa had no prejudice against Germans, but Gammy did, even though her mother came of German stock. Pa had no prejudice against Jews. Gammy did—in fact, Ken had warned me in advance not to speak of my mother's being Jewish. From the start, Gammy and I simply did not hit it off. I learned that she had wanted Ken to show interest in a married woman named "Ruthie" who lived in Michigan! Then he married me, to her disappointment. Needless to say, this wasn't exactly music to my ears!

Best Interpreter Gen. Lucius Clay Ever Had Says in 9 Languages That She Likes Wichita

It is a fine thing to hear the former Ellen Cremer of Stuttgart, Berlin, and other points in Germany, say she loves the United States, Kansas, and Wichita.

It is a fine thing to hear her say that she is amazed at the bustle and get-up-and-go of Americans, Kansans, and Wichitans. From her it's high praise, because she's full of bustle and get up and go, herself.

It is additionally interesting because she can say these pretty things in nine languages. These include English, Russian, German, French, Spanish, Portuguese, Italian, Modern Greek, and Armenian.

The former Miss Cremer is now Mrs. Kenneth L. Myers, 2137 South Minnesota, and even more important to her and her husband, a former U. S. army captain who proposed to her while he was dressed like Aunt Jemima, she's the mother of eight-month-old Kenneth, Jr., known around the four-room, fourplex apartment in which they live as "Twurp."

With General Clay

Mrs. Myers met her husband, an attorney from Broken Bow, Neb., while both were on the staff of General Lucius D. Clay, commandant of U. S. occupation government in Germany. General Clay said, in writing, that Mrs. Myers is the best interpreter he ever had.

One of her duties was to untangle for the general the Russian language, make it come out American with a broad "A." What the Russians had to say was rather important to the general, and still is to all Americans, everywhere.

Mrs. Myers has offered her services to the University of Kansas extension center, 212 South Market. The K. U. people are organizing, and Mrs. Myers will instruct, the only course in Russian in this part of the country. The class will begin its lessons early in February.

Mrs. Myers has plans, and the energy to carry them out, that would stagger most Americans, in spite of her protestations that our citizens are more vigorous.

To Teach Russian

She'll be a wife and mother. She'll teach Russian to K. U. extension students. She'll study for a degree from the University of Wichita, an

STANDS WITH THE GENERAL—Shown above with Gen. Lucius D. Clay is Ellen Cremer, of whom Clay said: "The finest interpreter I ever had."—(U. S. Army Signal Corps Photo.)

SINGS TO HER FAMILY—Shown above, right, is Mrs. Kenneth L. Myers, formerly Ellen Cremer, now of 2137 South Minnesota, with her husband and son, Kenneth, Jr. The song she is playing and singing is "Let the Rest of the World Go by," and young Kenneth seems to think his mother can sing as well as General Clay thinks she can interpret.—(Eagle Staff Photo.)

An excerpt from an article in *The Wichita Eagle* of January 28, 1950, just after we moved to Wichita with our first son, Kenny.

Our Own Home

WHEN Ken and I moved to Wichita, Kansas in January of 1950, I was very happy.

My husband, like his father a conservative thinker with keen interest in politics, declined a job offer in a large, politically liberal law firm and opened his own law office. He also earned money from a route of soft drink and candy vending machines. We bought our first home in December, 1950, just before our second child was born. By 1958 we had four boys and two girls, all healthy and bright. My childhood dream of a large family around the dinner table had come true.

Ken and I in 1955 with children Mark (b. 1954), Karen (b. 1952), Eddy (b. 1951), and Kenny (b. 1949). Inset: Christie (b. 1956) and John (b. 1958).

I augmented the family income by part-time foreign language teaching for the University of Kansas and Wichita State University. I was frequently invited to speak before civic and church groups about my life in Nazi Germany. I also took evening college courses. To quench my hunger for serious reading, I again began to devour philosophical writings.

We were materially successful, but spiritually these were our dry years. We attended a large church of my husband's denomination. Everything was the same as in Nebraska, except on a larger scale. In about 1958 we transferred to another church closer to our home. Ken found that it was politically and theologically liberal, which upset him greatly. The denomination's leadership embraced numerous socialist-communist causes during the Cold War.

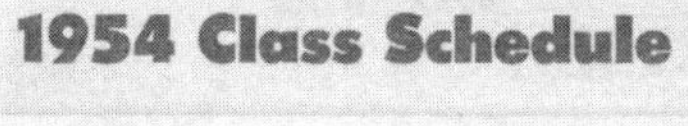

1954 Class Schedule

Invest a Few Hours in Your Future
attend
The Fall

ADULT EXTENSION CLASSES

arranged for you by

University of Kansas Extension Center
214-216 Derby Bldg.
Phone Fo 3-2725
3rd & Broadway Wichita 2, Kans.

- **FOREIGN LANGUAGES (Conversational)**

This Center will present two of the following Basic Conversational Language Courses: Spanish—Italian—Portuguese (Brazilian)—French—or Russian. These courses are designed to give you practical training in conversation. Textbooks will be used. Students completing the course will speak enough of the specific language for all every day requirements. If you are interested, be sure to ENROLL NOW, because the courses offered will be based on advance enrollments. An organizational meeting for all classes will be held in Room 214 Derby Buiding, 7:30 p.m., September 14. The first meetings of the classes will be held on Tuesday, September 21 and Thursday, September 23 at the 20th Century Club.

Tuesdays and Thursdays
7:30-9:30 p.m.
Organizational Meeting, Tuesday, September 14 at 214 Derby Building, 3rd & Broadway

Instructor: Mrs. Kenneth Myers
Place: 20th Century Club

15 meetings
Certificate
$15.00

A class schedule listing one of the foreign language courses I taught for the University of Kansas in the 1950's.

In 1958, at age 79, Pa was killed across the street from his home while returning from his office on his small motorcycle when he was struck by a drunk driver. Apart from wearing glasses and using a hearing aid in one ear, he was in good health right up to his death. He had received his law degree from Harvard and practiced law in Broken Bow all his life in the "Myers Building" which he had built and which still stands today near the center of the town.

After Pa died, Gammy liked it less and less in Broken Bow. Eventually she moved away to a property she had bought in Red Feather Lakes, Colorado. Although she was left well off after Pa's death, she spent more and more of her inheritance of several hundred thousand dollars, finally becoming quite poor. She then joined her sister Mamie, a retired school teacher, and they lived on Mamie's small pension plus social security. Frank, her son, also came to live with them. Around 1970 they moved to Spokane, Washington.

Meanwhile, our family was outgrowing our house, and so, in February of 1960, we moved to one with one more bedroom. By that time, Ken Jr., age 11, had taken up bassoon playing; Edwin Carl, 9, played the clarinet; Karen, 8, played the violin and the piano; Mark, 6, knew a song called "Indian Tom-Toms" which he hammered out fortissimo on the piano. Christie, 4, and John, 2, were distinguished by loud singing voices. (Christie eventually learned guitar, and John learned the trumpet.) Added to that was my good, loud talking voice. No wonder Ken separated his office from our home that year as well!

And God

THE most important event in my life was my conversion to Christ. It took place on July 10, 1960.

By 1960 I had become increasingly informed regarding the political deterioration of America and the threat from world communism. I also read extensively in the work of the French existentialist philosopher Jean-Paul Sartre. Sartre asserted that God does not exsist, and therefore there are no moral absolutes whatsoever; that life is "absurd" with no meaning other than to "authenticate oneself" by exercising total freedom. He gave this example: Suppose you want to cross a busy street in Paris, and next to you stands a frail old woman who also wants to get across. You can offer her your arm and safely guide her across. Fine! Or you can step behind her and push her under an oncoming truck. Fine, too! Either choice will "authenticate you."

I read this and I thought that I, too, did not believe in God. I realized that if there is no God, then indeed there are no moral absolutes. Everyone is "existentially free" and has a perfect right to do as he pleases, and this is the only "meaning" of life, an absurd struggle of all against all in which the strongest win. And if this is so, then Hitler simply and rightly "authenticated himself" by killing six million Jews including most of my mother's family in Poland!

But I couldn't accept this. I wanted a world with moral absolutes and real meaning, a world in which Hitler was wrong. If the world was as Sartre saw it—and as I saw it, too, since I did not believe in God—then why go on living? Why bring up children to live in such a world, especially if it would be ruled by communism? Why come all the way from Germany to the United States only to be caught up in Socialism-Communism? For some two months I considered killing all my children and Ken, and committing suicide. You see, I had merely seen America as a rich, comfortable, free place of convenience where something like Nazism "couldn't happen," and where it might be good to bring up children. Now I realized that America could be seduced, too.

But I did love my family. And I really *did* want to go on living if any sense and hope in life could be found. Only where on earth could I find sense and hope? Then Ken said, "Have you considered God?" And I remembered my father's telling Mother and me: "You must have faith in God!" ("Ihr muesst Gottvertruaen haben!" I can still hear him.) I also remembered the simple faith of Anna Thalheimer, the dear little crippled, Roman Catholic lady in who lived in the same rooming house as myself during WWII in Germany. She once pointed to a picture of Jesus Christ and told me, "*He* does it" (*He* gave her constant cheerfulness and perseverance in very difficult circumstances in wartime Nazi Germany). But how *could* I come to *Jesus Christ*? I did not believe He was God; He was just a man, a "great teacher." And because to me he was just another man, how could he "die for my sins" 2,000 years ago? Besides, why should he need to die for my sins? I wasn't such a wicked sinner anyway, but a pretty nice person! Surely at least 51% of my deeds were good and thus would get me into heaven (if there were such a place). I did not even believe in God as a Person Who can hear prayer, and I hadn't prayed for over 20 years.

But I was desperate, and Man could not help. All my own talents and efficiency in which I had prided myself could not help. It would take a God above men Who could hear and answer prayer. So on Thursday, July 7, 1960 I stood in our dining room where I am now writing this, and said in my heart, "God, if you are there and know what I am thinking right now—and if you truly are God, you must be able to do that—if you are the God my father spoke of, who gives joy in trouble, show me you exist, and also show me that Jesus Christ died for my sins."

That Sunday, July 10, 1960, I had a miserable experience as a substitute Sunday School teacher for a high school and college age, utterly unbelieving class at our church. I didn't want to use their extremely socialistic Sunday school lesson book, written by a Harvard professor who was a known Communist. So, when I arrived in the classroom, I looked around for what to do, and saw some old New Testaments sitting on a windowsill, covered with dust. There weren't enough for all the students. When I handed them out, the students began to chuckle and smirk. They thought I had walked in from Mars. The only passage in the Bible that I knew where to find was the Beatitudes in Matthew 6. The class hour was a terrible flop.

After this defeat, I didn't even want to attend the church service. I went to our car and drove out of the parking lot to get home. Just then, the thought came to me, "Ellen Myers, if Jesus lived today, and the communists took him and shot him; or if you were there when the mob in Jerusalem shouted, 'Crucify him,' you might not yell with the crowd to kill him, because you are too 'nice.' But you would not lift a finger to help him, either, even though you knew he was innocent, because to you Jesus is just another man for whom you would not risk your life, and you are a coward!" And instantly I remembered the Jew sweeping dust in the Stuttgart street in 1944, and how I did not help because I had been afraid of the people around me. Then it hit me: *Therefore Jesus would die for your sin—the sin of not doing what you knew to be right.*

This was the first time in my life I saw that "sin" isn't just doing wrong, but also *not* doing what is *right*! I did not know yet that this is taught in the Bible (Matthew 25:45, James 4:17). I instantly knew I was a sinner because sins of *omission* are sins just as much as sins of *commission*. I knew I had received the answer to my "thought"—really prayer!—of three days before. I knew there was a God, the absolutely trustworthy God of my father, and that He had heard me. I knew Jesus was God, the Bible was true, and my father was right. Life had absolute meaning with abolute "right" and "wrong" which nothing could ever change. Immediately my fear of the future and all thought of suicide fell away, never to return. I was suddenly filled with great joy.

I drove home in a daze. I came into our house and told my family, "Something has happened to me." It was my new birth, though I didn't know these words then. We found our Bible, and I took it off the shelf. I knew hardly anything about it anymore except that it told of God and Christ. I loved it. I loved my Father in Heaven Who had heard and answered my prayer. I loved my dear blessed Redeemer and Savior, my Lord and my God, Jesus Christ, Who died for me that I might live.

I knew I was a sinner. Since I could see that it was true that He died for my sins (you see, I had *never* accepted that before, rebelled against it, never even considered whether it *might* be true), then all the other Scriptures telling of his Father in Heaven and this His only begotten Son were true—were simply telling the *facts of life* as Moses and the prophets and the Apostles had experienced them as true. We read Genesis 1 that morning because it was the Bible's first chapter. Immediately, I clearly understood and accepted the fact of biblical creation, and the evolutionary teaching of the Nazi schools fell away. From then on I got up early in the morning for my quiet time with Bible reading and prayer. We had daily family Bible study. Dear Ken returned to Christ and all the children except the eldest came to know Him, too. After about seven or eight months we left our liberal church, persuading three other couples to leave also. We transferred to a non-denominational, Bible-believing church clear across town, with a strongly anti-communist young minister.

Thus I was found again, like the lost sheep. And true to His glorious words in the blessed Sermon on the Mount, my fear of the future fell away: "But seek ye first the kingdom of God, and his righteousness; and all these things shall be added unto you. Take no thought for the morrow: for the morrow shall take thought for itself." (Matthew 6:33-34) His joy has remained in me through my many good times and some severe trials. All in all, the years since my conversion to Christ on July 10, 1960 have been aptly described in the Bible:

> Blessed are they that dwell in thy house; they will be always praising thee. Blessed is the man whose strength is in thee; in whose heart are thy ways. *Who passing through the valley of tears make it a well;* and the pools are filled with water. They go from strength to strength, each appears before God in Zion.
>
> Psalm 84:4-7

Life is Family

FROM the fall of 1960 to the spring of 1967, I taught at Wichita Collegiate School. Its first headmaster was Mr. Bill Hemmer. He was followed in 1963 by Mr. Randall Storms, who stayed in the post for almost 25 years. Collegiate's principal founder was Robert D. Love, president of the Love Box Company here in Wichita.

I taught French from Kindergarten up through all grades, and also Latin I and II in Grades 7 and 8. I was paid I think $75 a month, and more importantly, the five youngest of our six children could attend for free. We welcomed this arrangement, because the public schools were already greatly deteriorating. We had realized how far away from Christian teaching and thorough academic instruction they had strayed.

Scholastically, Collegiate was excellent then, as I suppose now. Its goal was to prepare its students for prestigious universities. The students came and still come from Wichita's wealthiest families, our social elite. Tuition is affordable only to them. Spiritually there has always been conflict between the secular and Christian elements at Collegiate. This conflict was already very much in evidence when I taught there, and eventually I stopped teaching there due to this circumstance. I opposed a number of non-Christian trends there. For example, I had to present true biblical Christianity to senior high school students in their French class in opposition to the false portrayal of the Christian faith in their French textbook.

Mr. Storms' son, Randy, whom I remember well as a shy little boy with big, sad eyes in my first and second grade classes, is now the much beloved and capable youth pastor at our Central Christian Church. As a young man, he became a commited, Bible-believing Christian after a horrible diving accident which paralyzed most of his body. God gave him a wonderful wife, Suzie, and a family with her two children from an earlier marriage. I love them all very much.

One beautiful addition to my Christian life came to me there at Collegiate. I found a long article about the famous French scientist Blaise Pascal (1623-1662) in a magazine which the library was going to discard. Pascal described our Lord's Presence with him on the night of November 23, 1654 in a handwritten sheet of paper found sewn in a seam of his coat after his death. This document is now widely known as the "Pascal Memorial." He wrote in part, "God of Abraham, God of Isaac, God of Jacob, Not the God of philosophers and learned men, Certitude, Certitude, feeling joy peace…" So I had felt, after meeting our Lord July 10, 1960. Pascal's life was radically changed; his book *Pensees* are a profound witness to our faith. Oh, how I loved his "Memorial"! I kept a copy of it in my purse until I gave it many years later to a professor of philosophy at Wichita State University who asked me about it.

I still run into some of my former students now and then. Many have become believers and thank me for helping them come to Christ.

During the '60's we also kept very active in informing ourselves and others of the truth about collectivist, godless communism and socialism. Hence we wrote letters to men in public office, leaders of public opinion, friends and acquaintances. We read and distributed a great many books, showed informative films, and took active interest in local and national election campaigns.

Ken continued in law and patriotic work. In 1963 he helped form the Conservative Party of Kansas of which I was elected vice-chairman. In 1964 Ken ran for Governor on the on the Kansas Conservative Party's ticket. With only a token campaign he was gratified to receive 12,000 votes! That Fall we worked hard for Barry Goldwater's presidential campaign.

In 1963 I wrote my second published novel, *Reprobate Silver*. The title is taken from Jeremiah 6:30: "Reprobate silver shall men call them, because the Lord has rejected them." It was a story based on true events in the 1930-1960 period and was heavily footnoted. It was set on a Midwestern college campus and dealt with people accepting or rejecting Christ. It was published in 1969 in magazine form by Christianity on Campus, a Christian college campus ministry. I hoped it would lead intellectual unbelievers, like myself before my conversion, to Christ.

One of my major concerns at that time was the salvation of my mother. I had always sensed the difference in faith between her and my father, and now I understood that he had known the Lord as I now did, but she never had.

After the end of World War II and the American occupation of our part of Germany, my parents were in a good position to resume working in their professions, of course, being absolutely untainted with Nazi connections. However, my father, 70 years old in 1946, crippled and with poor eyesight, could not do too much professional work any more. My mother, however, eagerly sought professional use for her pent-up energy and talents. Eventually she worked as the chief editor of a magazine she founded and got an important German publishing house (I think the Deutsche Verlagsanstalt in Stuttgart) to back it. It was named "Die Landfrau"—*The Farm Woman.*

My mother and father remained in Germany, where my father died of a stroke on Christmas Eve of 1953. A few years after this, my mother became acquainted with two young Mormon "missionaries" and found a way to come to America under the sponsorship of the Mormon Church. She stopped editing her magazine, relocated to Salt Lake City, Utah, and worked there in the Mormon Genealogical Institute (where Mormons from all over the world can have a search made for their non-Mormon ancestors so they can be baptized on their ancestors' behalf). I do not believe she really accepted the tenets of the Mormon Church, though she did become a member of it for several years. Our children and I visited her in Salt Lake City for several successive summers. After I became a Christian, I would try to win her to Christ, but without success. Once she told me, "I wouldn't even listen to you about this, but you have changed."

In the summer of 1964 she fell very ill with cancer of the uterus. A hysterectomy was performed in St. Luke's Hospital in Salt Lake City, but the doctor took me aside and told me the cancer had spread all over her body, and that she had perhaps a few more months to live. He said he had not told her of this because he feared her terrible outbursts of anger.

In August 1964 she came to Wichita to die. We had her stay in one of the rental apartments which we then owned near our home. She was rapidly declining. I remember how she gave me a collection of American silver coins which she had owned for years; to me this was a most significant sign that she realized the end was near. She telephoned her brother, Leon Ruslender, who came and visited overnight, but could offer no other help. Then she became unable to keep any food down. We took her to St. Francis Hospital. A day or two later, I drove to visit her there, praying all the way there that she might come to the Lord. I came to her hospital room. For the first time ever, she asked me to pray for her. I immediately thought of James 1:5-7, which I then read to her in German:

> If any of you lack wisdom, let him ask of God, that giveth to all men liberally, and upbraideth not, and it shall be given him. But let him ask in faith, nothing wavering. For he that wavereth is like a wave of the sea driven with the wind and tossed. For let not that man think that he shall receive any thing of the Lord.

Suddenly a great radiant smile transfigured my mother's face. She said, "It's so simple! Why didn't I see it before? It's so simple!" Then she picked up the phone by her bedside and called my husband, at home with the children, and told him, "I am a Christian too now!" What a joy! Had I not been there when she came to Christ, I might not have believed that she did. How good our Father in Heaven was to bring it to pass like this!

She lived with us still for a very little while, but died on September 19, 1964 in Wesley Hospital. She had requested earlier that her body be cremated, and with some reluctance we complied with this request. Later her ashes were sent to Germany to my good friend Laura Stark in Neckarsulm, who had them interred beside my father's grave in the Catholic cemetery of Allfeld, located near our former farm in Kreis (county) Mosbach, Baden, Germany.

She was a most remarkable woman with many diverse facets in her personality. Doubtless her ability to master foreign languages came down to me and my children, as did her love of music, especially music in a minor key. She was a most interesting conversationalist. She had great ability in mathematics, and would sometimes spend hours of leisure to solve math problems "just for fun." I've already mentioned her physical courage. She always wanted to be the center of attention, and loved to tell in detail of occasions when she had offensively, sarcastically, or rudely contradicted or corrected others in public at social get-togethers. Her ways of relating won her respect from others but not their liking. She brooked no contradiction or questioning, wanting to be in control of all circumstances of her life at all times. It was an impossible goal, but she did not recognize this until almost the very end of her life.

From the mid-1960s on, our oldest son, Kenny, rebelled against Christ and us, causing Ken and I great grief. He was always Gammy's favorite, so she took his side against Ken and me. She financed a trip to a Belgian music school against our wish; he left it on his own as he had earlier given up his music scholarship at Juilliard Music School in New York. After years of drifting from country to country and belief to belief, he finally stabilized in Switzerland, and became a Swiss citizen. There he married a Muslim nurse/midwife from Benin, Africa, adopted the Muslim faith himself, and settled down in comfortable economic circumstances with two adopted sons. I am praying every day for his salvation, trusting our Father in Heaven to answer.

In December of 1965, Ken had a heart attack and was hospitalized until just after the Christmas holidays. During Ken's months of slow but steady recovery, our son, Ed, took care of the vending business after school hours. Within a few months everything pretty well returned to normal, with Ken putting in full days again.

When our son, John, was 8 in 1966, he fell and cut his hand deeply just before a swimming race. He went on to win a "First" with his relay team–and had stitches taken immedately *after* the meet!

I should mention here that Ken and I have always had good relations with black people. When Ken operated his vending machine route, a black man named King Ingram worked for him for years. Many of Ken's legal clients were black, and Ken typically charged them fees far below the "going rate." Ken's black friends included, among many others, a Captain Russell, with whom Ken worked in the Army Reserves. Our neighborhood, which was completely white in the 1950's, became almost completely black by the 70's. I love my black neighbors, am grateful for the many Christians among them, and get along with them very well.

In early 1968 Ken and I had an opportunity to visit Florida. This was the time when we were invited to inspect some "retirement properties" around Fort Myers, Florida. We found out we did not really want to spend our old age in a Florida retirement community! However, we had a great time for several days, and we even drove across Florida by the wonderful highway across the Everglades to visit my Uncle Leon, an older brother of my mother's, and his wife, Aunt Fannie, in Miami. My aunt asked me in detail about my Christian faith, saying that she could see I had changed. "You looked hard when you visited us in Washington in 1948," she said, "you look softer and gentler now--that's why I asked you about your new faith." She and my uncle died shortly afterwards. I can only hope that they received Christ.

Trial

A FEW weeks after our lovely Florida trip, we found out I was pregnant. We were delighted with the news! Our physician was Dr. Leonard Podrebarac, whose young sons I had taught at Wichita Collegiate School, and whose wife, Hildegard, was German-born like myself.

In the third month of this pregnancy I began to bleed. We called Dr. Podrebarac, and he said I was probably miscarrying. He said his wife had recently had a miscarriage, which had not presented any major trouble; so he advised us just to have me rest in bed, and after the baby had been passed, I would quickly recover.

However, my miscarriage turned out to be life-threatening. I bled more and more heavily. There was no pain, only this rushing flow, which would increase at my slightest motion, even just lifting a hand. The family put many layers of newspapers on the bed on which I rested so the blood wouldn't soak through the bedding. I would feel big clots of blood about to pass and try to make it to the bathroom for them; soon I felt so weak that Ken and the boys would have to almost carry me there and back. Then I just lay there on the bed as quietly as possible.

I realized I might die when too much blood had drained from my body. Previously I had been afraid of death. But now there was no fear, just great gentleness surrounding me. (I have never been afraid of death since then, for Jesus will be there with me when it comes.) My mind was slowly becoming blank, except for the Name—"Jesus, Jesus. I will be with You soon, and I want to go."

"But what about my family, my good husband and six children? They still need me here."

Then the thought came to me urgently: "You need to go to the hospital and have a blood transfusion." I believe it came directly from Jesus.

I told Ken that I needed to go to the hospital and have a blood transfusion. We had no health insurance for me. But my husband called an ambulance to get me to St. Francis Hospital. Soon they came and took me there. As they unloaded me from the ambulance stretcher to the hospital stretcher, a young man tried to take my pulse and heartbeat. He couldn't find any! He was visibly very concerned. When I later told this to a friend, who was a doctor's wife, she exclaimed, "No heartbeat! You were techincally dead!"

I was rushed to an emergency room where my blood pressure was checked (no blood pressure!) and they tested some blood. That test came back as OK. Then Dr. Podrebarac came in, took one look at me (I must have looked very pale) and asked that the blood test be repeated. This time it indicated that a blood transfusion was needed, even before an emergency D&C could be performed. I received three pints of blood all in all and then quickly recovered.

We lost a dear baby that day. Even yet I haven't totally stopped grieving over this loss, and I expect to see this child (I think of it as a boy whom I call David in my heart, but of course it may be a much welcomed daughter) in heaven.

In 1969 another much desired baby was on the way. After a stormy pregnancy our little Becky was born December 31, 1969. Our doctor told me she was "mongoloid," at that time the common name for Down Syndrome. Now, all my life I had dreaded a mentally retarded child as the worst disaster that might happen to me. My husband consulted a medical encyclopedia we then had in our home. The entry for "mongoloid" read, "These little idiots are best put into an institution before you get attached to them." My husband said angrily, "She is our little girl and we will keep her!" He shut the book with a bang and threw it on the floor, and, later, into the trash!

However, that night in the hospital I looked closely at Becky and saw the small head, the slanted eyes, the broad neck, the small hands with their "simian" (ape-like) single crease in the palms, all confirming she was abnormal. The thought came into my mind that during the night when she was left with me I could place my pillow over her face, myself over the pillow, suffocate her and later claim it had happened by accident. Then I remembered Matthew 25:40: "As you have done it to the least of these my brethren, you have done it to Me." I could not suffocate Jesus! And Becky was Jesus to me in that moment.

The next weeks were very hard. Becky was very apathetic, even nursing much less than seemed right. I took care of her from a sense of duty, but without affection. Inwardly I wrestled with God. "How could you do this to me," I raged. "I wanted to do an extra special good job raising this first child born after I became a Christian! Why did you do this to me when you knew it was the thing I dreaded most in life?!" Frequently I would go outside, sit in our car, and cry.

Yet I knew He was right there with me. I sensed Him telling me that He could not let me know now why He had done this; if He told me now, I would not believe it, and it would not accomplish His purpose. He also gave me a Bible verse to which I clung through these weeks. It was Isaiah 63:9, "In all their afflictions He was afflicted, and the angel of His presence saved them. In His love and mercy He redeemed them; He lifted them up and carried them all the days of old." I knew He grieved with me.

Finally, about six weeks later, on a day when Becky had lain in her little bed motionless for 13 hours, not once waking up even to nurse, I could not bear it any longer. That night, sleepless in bed, I remembered Psalm 55:22: "Cast thy burden upon the Lord, and He will sustain thee." I cried out to Him: "I cannot carry this burden any more! Keep Your promise! Take it and sustain me!" Immediately, it seemed as though a burden was physically lifted from me and taken up out of sight. I felt totally relieved, and also totally reconciled to having this child. My care for her became much more than duty; I now loved her from the heart. Now she became responsive to me, smiled, cooed, and thrived.

A story in a devotional book by dear Pastor Richard Wurmbrand often comforted me in the first hard weeks after Becky's birth (and later) when I still grieved over her Down Syndrome: Cathy lived for twenty years in a home for retarded children. She never spoke a word, but either gazed quietly at the walls or made disordered movements. To eat, to drink, to sleep, were her whole life. She didn't seem to participate at all in what went on around her. Eventually, one of her legs had to be amputated.

One day the doctor called the director of the home to come quickly. Cathy was dying. When they entered the room together, they could hardly believe their ears. Cathy was singing Christian hymns she had heard (and must have picked up), just those suitable for one approaching death! She repeated again and again the German song, "Where does the soul find its home, its rest?" She sang for half an hour with a transfigured face, and then passed quietly away.

As God willed, the German song mentioned above was my own favorite song when I was a little child. Here it is:

Wo findet die Seele die Heimat, die Ruh,
Wer deckt sie mit schutzenden Fittichen zu?
Ach, bietet die Welt Keine Heimstatt mir an,
Wo Sunde nicht herrschen, nicht anfechten Kann?
Nein nein---nein, nein, hier ist sie nicht,
Die Heimat der Seele ist droben im Licht!

The following poem has comforted me many times during our sweet Becky's life, as has Psalm 68:19: "Praise be to the Lord, Who daily bears our burdens (or, daily loads us with benefits), the God who is our salvation."

HEAVEN'S VERY SPECIAL CHILD

A meeting was held quite far from Earth,
It's time again for another birth.
Said the angels to the Lord above,
This special child will need much love.

He may not run, or laugh, or play,
His thoughts may seem quite far away.
In many ways he won't adapt,
And he'll be known as handicapped.

So let's be careful where he's sent,
We want his life to be content,
Please, Lord, find the people who
Will do a special job for you.

They will not realize right away
The leading role they're asked to play.
But with this child sent from above
Comes stronger faith and richer love.

And soon they'll know the privilege given
In caring for this gift from heaven.
Their precious charge, so meek and mild
Is heaven's special child.

–Edna Massimilla

Ken celebrated his 60th birthday on Thanksgiving Day, November 23, 1972. I was very happy because everything was well, especially with our little Becky. I knelt in our dining room and thanked our Father for her. I added this: "Please, when something else happens that I think is very terrible, don't let me be angry with you this time as I was at first after Becky was born, but let me remember this moment and understand that you mean it all for good."

Ken, Becky, and I in late 1970.

Early Saturday morning, November 25, 1972, Ken got up and covered Becky, whose baby bed was in our bedroom, with a blanket. I went to the bathroom. When I returned, I found him lying on the floor between our beds. I knew immediately that he was dead. I yelled, "No, no, no!" Ed woke up and came down from upstairs. Soon Karen and John, who had been throwing John's newspaper route together, came back. I called for an ambulance and they came and took Dad to St. Francis hospital. I followed in our car. A doctor examined him and said he had died from a massive heart attack (his second).

My first thought was sad: we could not celebrate our 25th wedding anniversary the following July. My next thought was glad:

Ken, the real Ken, was in Heaven with Jesus now. My next thought was thanks: we had parted as loving husband and wife, with nothing between us that either of us needed to forgive the other for. What a good husband and father Ken had always been! I remembered my prayer of two days before and knew this, too, was in God's good will. I also knew fairly certainly right away that I would never marry again; Jesus Christ was now directly "my Husband and Head" (in the words of a song I wrote then).

The day of the funeral was sunny and mild. It took place at Broadway Funeral Home. My worst moment was passing by the open coffin and seeing the face of the corpse all stiff and made up, so different than my living husband. A dear friend, Pastor Ken Peterson of Calvary Bible Church, officiated at the funeral. He stood by my side and whispered, "The real Ken is in Heaven with Jesus now." This truth comforted me very much. Ken's grave is in Old Mission Cemetary at 21st and Hillside. To this day, I miss him and remember him with love and gratitude. Below is a copy of his biography given to Pastor Peterson before the funeral:

KENNETH L. MYERS

Kenneth L. Myers was born on November 23, 1912 in Broken Bow Nebraska, a county seat (about 4,500 in population) in central Nebraska. His father, Edwin F. Myers, was an attorney and lifelong student of economics and politics. Kenneth was the second of four brothers, of whom only one now survives. He graduated from high school and worked his way through Harvard University, majoring in economics and government, and graduating in 1934. He was admitted to the Nebraska Bar in 1935 and practiced law with his father until the outbreak of World War II.

During World War II he served in the European Theater, rising from Private to Captain. He was wounded in action (shrapnel in the leg) during the Battle of the Bulge and received the Purple Heart. From 1946-1948 he served in the U. S. Military Government in Germany, first in Berlin, and later in Stuttgart. It was there that he met his future wife, Ellen Cremer, who was then employed as an interpreter for General Lucius D. Clay and members of his staff dealing with top German government officials. Kennneth and Ellen were married on July 2, 1948 in Stuttgart and then returned to America, first to Ken's hometown. In 1949 they moved to Wichita where they made their home ever since, until

Kenneth died of heart failure in the morning of November 25, 1972, just two days after having celebrated his 60th birthday on Thanksgiving Day 1972. Six of Kenneth's seven children were born in St. Francis Hospital in Wichita (the eldest son was born in Broken Bow, Nebraska on May 17, 1949).

Kenneth practiced law and owned a small vending business. He belonged to the U. S. Army active Reserves, 89th Division, in Wichita, until 1966 when he retired with the rank of Lt. Colonel. He was a member of the Reserve Officers' Association and VFW Post 112 until his death.

He was a founding member of the Conservative Party of Kansas and served as its legal council. He was the Conservative Party's candidate for Governor of Kansas in 1964, and Attorney General in 1966. His deep concern for the internal and international security of our country, which originated mainly and immediately after World War II as Communism took over country after country, was at the root of his strong and abiding involvement in this political movement. Moved by the same concern, he joined the John Birch Society, for which he served as volunteer coordinator for several years, and of which he remained a member until his death.

Kenneth knew that the internal and external dangers threatening our country could not have grown so much, had it not been for a pre-existing moral decline and abandonment of God's law within our country. The legalization of abortion, that is, of the killing of "unwanted" human beings, was to him a sign of how far this moral decline had gone. He became an active member of Kansas Right to Life to help reverse this trend, and although in failing health since a heart attack in 1965 and recurrent ulcer and stomach trouble, continued his active work with the Conservative Party, and encouraged his wife to devote much of her time to Kansas Right to Life and to accept that organization's nomination of her as president in 1972.

Kenneth Myers was a commited Christian who never missed an opportunity to witness to his belief in Christ and the Bible. But beyond his spoken witness, he endeavored to let his whole life, day by day, be a testimony to our Living God, His Law and His grace. Unless so ill that he had to be bedfast, he worked conscienciously day in and day out, his law office being open for appointments at almost any hour. On principle, he lived frugally and unostentatiously. His time and his income were freely given for causes and people he believed deserving.

He was an inwardly happy man, usually whistling a little tune, and content with simple pleasures: a picnic, going shopping with his wife or children, going on a fishing trip or an occasional hunting trip. One family highlight would be Dad Ken's taking out all the family plus friends to a local restaurant for an inexpensive but comfortable dinner. All his free time was spent with his family. He was very happy with his littlest daughter, Becky, now nearly three years old, and would picture future trips with his wife and Becky, perhaps camping.

Kenneth was very eager for his children to learn to play musical instruments, and would sometimes tell his wife that one big reason he had married her was her playing the piano and accordion and singing, because this would insure the children's playing and singing, too. And it did!

He was always eager to hear what his children were doing, to share in their problems and joys. He was very hospitable and easy to talk to. He encouraged his children to choose their own profession without regard to worldly status or wealth. One of his many wonderful character traits was that he never despised or shunned manual or "dirty" labor. He took care of the daily cleanup and repair of several soft drink vending machines for some 15 years before turning the work over to his sons. He taught his children by word and life that all honest work is good in God's sight and "respectable."

Among the organizations he supported were [the forerunner of Summit Ministries of Manitou Springs, Colorado]; the Southwest Radio Church of the Air, of Oklahoma City; and Jesus to the Communist World [now Voice of the Martyrs], founded by Richard Wurmbrand. He had a lifelong interest in farming, having farmers and ranchers among his relatives and friends. He had been looking for a small farm property to buy for his retirement, but had not found any before his untimely death.

At the time of Ken's death I was left with six children still at home. One by one the older ones left, married and had their own families. I had been extremely active in the developing pro-life movement, traveling all over our state as a speaker, with Ken along to drive and watch Becky. I would speak to about two groups per week, educating them against abortion and "mercy killing" ("active" euthanasia). Now that Ken was gone, this was no longer possible, though I never stopped pro-life work altogether.

Through Patience and Comfort

IN 1973, we were happy to join what would be our church home for a number of years—the Anglican Orthodox Church. This denomination, founded in 1963, was true to our Risen Lord and Saviour, His Word, in true Christian love opposing apostasy (Jude 22-23), social revolution (I Timothy 6:1-11), and the "new morality" (really the old immorality–I Corinthians 6:15-20). We opened an Anglican Mission/Chapel in Wichita at Ken's former office in a house we owned on Hillside St.

In June of 1974, I, along with Christie, John, and Becky attended the national Convention of the Anglican Orthodox Church in Statesville, North Carolina. It was a blessed experience in every way. By that time our local mission had grown to full-fledged "church" status. I was the secretary and organist for the church. Truly God had been very good to us in everything!

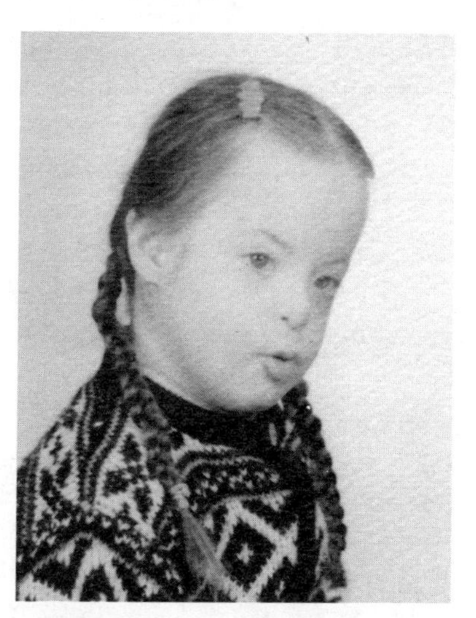

Becky as a pre-schooler.

In 1974 dear little Becky began attending pre-school three mornings a week. She also took swimming lessons at the central "Y" and swam well with great joy. It was surely a blessing for us all to have this little one in our home!

A few years before Ken's death, Gammy and Ken's younger brother, Frank, became followers of a Mr. George Hamilton, a man who held sort of a New Age worldview. Mr. Hamilton also seemed to be an accomplished "con man." Gammy and Frank gave him more and more money. Finally, they gave him a $38,000 mortgage on the farm property which had been the homestead of the Myers family, near Lexington, Nebraska. Hamilton contacted Ken and proposed that Ken pay him $15,000. In return, Hamilton would release the mortgage and deed on the farm to Ken and me. Hamilton really had to do this because Ken held a small part of the title to the farm. I had just sold the German farm inherited from my mother, so I had $15,000 cash in the bank. This was used to conclude the deal with this man. Ken and I became the legal co-owners of the farm. After Ken's death in 1972, I was able to sell the farm for substantially more to a Lexington farmer, Esa Maloley.

In 1974, I believe at the end of May, I received a phone call from the sheriff's office in Spokane, Washingtion. I was told that Gammy, Mamie Haumont (Gammy's sister), and Frank Myers had been discovered dead in a parked car in Spokane. The car had been rigged with a hose from the exhaust pipe into the car, so the three had died from inhalation of carbon monoxide. No papers were found on them except a birthday card I had sent to Gammy for her birthday on May 18, and this is how the sheriff's people located me. They were buried in the Broken Bow cemetary in either the Haumont or the Myers family lots. I think Gammy and Frank planned this joint suicide, and poor Mamie went along with them without realizing what was to happen.

More could be said about Gammy, but I don't have the heart for it. I remember her as a very slender, gracious, well-dressed lady with excellent taste in interior decoration, a great cook and meticulous seamstress. When Ken and I lived at the Myers residence in Nebraska, I was young, and not yet a Christian believer. I did not have the discernment to see that she must have been always discontented and unhappy, with unfulfilled longings for beautiful surroundings and the cultural events of a large city instead of tiny Broken Bow, forlorn on the prairie wilderness. Pa had far more inner resources and thus seemed sturdier in spirit. They were not congenial at all. The church they attended all their lives, already estranged from the Bible but so socially acceptable still in the American rural midwest gave no help. I think Gammy adopted a "New Age" spirituality years before I met her. Her library held many books by Agnes Sanford, a forerunner of that spirituality. Hers is a sad story, along with the story of her sons, and less so, the story of Pa, her husband.

At age six, Little Becky transferred to special education classes at Fabrique School. She was an affectionate and trusting little girl, joyful and a blessing to all who knew her, especially to her family!

Our dear heavenly Father and Jesus never left me without the knowledge of their love and presence. Countless times I have been especially strengthened. One particular instance of God's amazing comfort stands out. On November 25, 1977, my second daughter eloped to Oklahoma City with a very unsuitable young man. This was the fifth anniversary of Ken's death and always a day of sad memory for me. Now it was doubly sad, for I doubted very much that this man would be a good husband to Christie, but was powerless to do anything about it. (To see a beloved child in terrible trouble and not be able to help them is a heartrending grief indeed.)

About two weeks later, on Tuesday, December 12, I got up early as usual to study my Bible. I read Psalm 84 and came to verses 5-7:

> Blessed is the man whose strength is in thee; in whose heart are the ways of them,
>
> Who passing through the valley of Baca [that is 'weeping'] make it a well; the rain also filleth the pools.
>
> They go from strength to strength, every one of them in Zion appeareth before God.

I wept, thinking of Christie. I wrote in the margin of my Bible: "Let me make this valley a well, Father" and dated it 12-12-77.

And right then, at about seven in the morning, the telephone rang. Who could it be this early? A woman said she was Mary Meyer in Chapman, Kansas. She asked whether I was the Ellen Myers who was active in the Right to Life movement. I said, "Yes." She then explained that I had spoken on the Right to Life about a year and a half earlier in her Catholic church in Chapman. The church had started a prayer circle which had been meeting weekly, Monday evenings, since then. From time to time, they had also been praying for me. "And last night," Mary Meyer said, "the Lord put it very urgently on our hearts to pray for you; and the Lord told me this morning to call you to tell you that He loves you abundantly, and that in the matter you now grieve about all will be well in the end."

I wrote this down in my Bible, too. God Himself, our dear Heavenly Father, loved me and cared for me so much that He let me know it in this amazing way. He Himself was my well of joy and salvation as He says in Isaiah 12:3: "Therefore with joy shall ye draw water out of the wells of salvation." And since that time, God has worked in Christie's life in many definite ways.

Yes, He knows all things. Yes, He loves us and cares for us. Yes, He may even use our brothers and sisters in Jesus to comfort us with special, miraculous comfort in our "valley of weeping." Thank you again, dear Father and Jesus!

In the Summer of 1980, I visited Germany, Switzerland, England, and France for a month, renewing old friendships. I was amazed at the changes—and in some ways, lack of changes—which had taken place there since I moved to America in 1948 (with no visits at all in between). I visited my friend, Laura, in Germany, and saw Kenny in Switzerland as well.

Becky continued her schooling at Fabrique School. She was now the "littlest one" at age 11, in a group of special ed teenagers, and therefore often "acted like a teenager," saying things like, "I want my privacy," or, "That's not good manners!"

In the Spring of 1982, Becky participated in the statewide Special Olympics and won a bronze medal in the 100-meter dash!

In 1983, Becky's pictures were submitted to a regional special ed art exhibit. She won a ribbon in Bowling at the Special Olympics that year as well.

God Our Maker

THE day I accepted Christ as my Savior, my involvement in the creation/evolution battle began. It was on that morning that we read Genesis, Chapter 1, as a family in our living room. As we read it, I realized that this part of God's Word did not agree with evolution! God would not have begun His Word with a lie or an error!

Soon I began to read the Christian creationist literature available at that time, and thus I must have been among the first to read the famous book *The Genesis Flood* by Drs. Henry Morris and John Whitcomb, published in 1961 and marking the beginning of the modern creation movement. In 1963 I became a subscriber to a new creationist publication intended for pastors and scientists, the *Bible Science Newsletter*. It was edited and published by Rev. Walter Lang (Lutheran Church, Missouri Synod) in Caldwell, Idaho and later in Minnesota. Rev. Lang also started the Bible-Science Association which promoted local chapters. The group is now called "Creation Moments" and no longer has local chapters.

In 1975, three years after Ken's death, I helped establish a chapter of the Bible-Science Association in Wichita. From 1978 on, the chapter was headed by Dr. Paul Ackerman, professor of psychology at Wichita State University, and a brave and persevering fighter for the truth of the Bible. Under Paul's leadership we have a Bible-Science Fellowship which continues to meet monthly.

I recognized that the creation/evolution issue is basic to the entire Christian faith and to all other cultural issues, an insight now shared by many top Christian defenders of the faith. In the 1970s there were only a few of us! I praise our Lord for creation pioneers like Dr. Henry Morris and Duane Gish, and also Dr. David Noebel, president of Summit Ministries, who saw this fundamental truth from the start of his work.

Almost from the beginning of the Bible-Science chapter in Wichita, I began to operate a free lending library of creationist materials from our home, knowing that due to Becky I could not work away from home—another purpose of God in giving Becky to us. I began to lend books and audio tapes, but then as now not many people take the trouble to inform themselves through books and audio tapes! Later there were more and more filmstrips, which were more in demand. But the library really began to flourish with the advent of the VHS format video cassettes. Thus for some 20 years I have been busy with creationist videos—acquiring them, publicizing them, lending them out all over the countrty by mail, and keeping track of them! Sometimes I send out as many as five in a day, and the work requires hours of work weekly. What a wonderful, rewarding task! I trust this has contributed to the spreading and deepening of trust in God's word "from the very first verse."

The library was the "Bible-Science Association Library" till 1997 and then renamed the "Creation Resource Library." In 1999 Paul Abramson, a friend in Berkeley, California, learned about the library and put our entire resource catalog on the internet! (www.creationism.org/library) Demand continues steady. Our Lord has always had His hand on the resources, for in all the years since its start the library has lost perhaps a dozen cassettes, and a few more have broken. I don't think I have lost any money, because borrowers usually send a bit of money to help with my postage/expenses. From time to time generous friends have contributed videos, books, etc., to the library. It has been a very joyful labor for us all!

In 1977, Paul Ackerman and I helped found the Creation Social Science and Humanities Society (CSSHS), and until 1994 we served as chief officers of this group. Together we published the *Social Science and Humanities Quarterly*. Through the Quarterly, my earlier studies of philosophy, history, and literature, now integrated with my Christian world view, bore fruit. Circulation was always small (about 800 maximum), but there were subscribers all around the world. I have a complete set of issues in a box in my basement.

The Quarterly was directed to people with a college background. We had hoped for many more subscribers among the faculties and students of Christian universities and colleges. In this we were sorely disappointed from the start. We learned the hard way, through several fruitless mass mailings, that "Christian" universities and colleges today are mostly compromising with evolution. However, we had a small number of dedicated, faithful subscribers and contributors. I still correspond with some of them today. This enterprise helped us become informed on a great number of issues in the social sciences and humanities. It also helped prepare me for my present work as a teacher at home and in church (e.g., "Understanding the Times" courses). Mr. Abramson put many articles from the *Quarterly* on his internet website, www.creationism.org Thus the information we gleaned and published may still help others by God's grace.

In 1981 the State of Arkansas passed a law mandating the "Two-Model Approach" to the teaching of origins, i.e., that both the evolution and creation models of origins should be taught. The evolutionist establishment was furious! A lawsuit was brought in Arkansas, with the ACLU, of course, attacking the new law as being against "the separation of church and state." As part of its legal strategy the ACLU sued to compel a whole host of creationist organizations, both large and small, to turn over all their financial statements, membership lists, correspondence, etc., to the ACLU! This was an absurdly wide "fishing expedition." Our little CSSHS was included in the suit.

The first I knew of this was one Friday afternoon. I was here at my dining room table when there was a knock at the door. When I opened the door, here stood a smooth young man in a three-piece suit, introducing himself as Attorney X (I forget his name) from the prestigious Wichita law firm of Foulson, Siefkin, et al. He handed me a big legal envelope containing a subpoena for producing in court all the CSSHS's records on finances, membership, "significant statements," published documents, etc. *on the following Wednesday*. He smirked and said, "That'll be the first time *this* has happened to you!" I answered, "You will hear from my lawyer. Good-bye."

Where to get a lawyer between Friday afternoon and the following Wednesday? I called a couple of men reputed to be "conservative." They did not want to touch it. Finally I called our old family lawyer, Earl Moore, who had handled my husband's will. He was the oldest practicing attorney in the state of Kansas at that time, well into his 80s. Dear Earl was old in body but not at heart! "Oh yes, I will take care of this," he said. "The first thing to do is to get a continuance so I can study the matter." And he did. The court hearing—before Judge Patrick Kelly, known as "left-wing," and himself a member of the ACLU (obviously the ACLU felt secure with him)—was postponed for three weeks.

The ACLU flew in a "big gun" lawyer from New York for the hearing. Earl Moore felt this was a false step. "Judge Kelly doesn't like bigwigs from New York flying to tell him how to run his court," he said. But Mr. Bigwig came in, complete with a very lengthy "brief". And praise the Lord! Judge Kelly completely rejected it! He called the ACLU action "a fishing expedition" and said they could get the CSSHS documents only if the Arkansas court sent an official court order to that effect. Earl Moore and I had won!

I did not actually go to court to observe all this, but it is in the court proceedings file in my filing cabinet ("Arkansas Lawsuit"). Instead, I spent the time at Wichita State University, handing out creationist materials from our free literature table. It turned out that we were the *only* creationist organization which had to give the ACLU no documents whatsoever.

If I had been ordered to surrender the documents, I had planned to call a press conference, go to the Sedgwick County Courthouse front steps, hand out a prepared statement for publication and set fire to all the documents. I might have gone to prison for it (I also would have refused to pay a fine). My dear Karen and her husband, Rick, would have taken care of Becky. But praise our Lord, Judge Kelly came out on our side! To his credit I also want to record that a little later he called me privately on the telephone and said he had thought the ACLU demand completely unjustified. And this from a man who had had some political run-ins with dear Ken in previous years!

Waiting to receive my B.A. from Wichita State University, May, 1983.

School Days Again

FROM 1978 to 1986 I finished undergraduate work and my M.A., both in history, at Wichita State University. I graduated Summa Cum Laude. In the Fall of 1985 I received the annual John Rydjord Award for graduate students. At first, I also took philosophy and had numerous run-ins with one especially militant atheist professor, Dr. P. I learned that the Christian worldview is well able to defend itself and defeat its enemies, and that worldly philosophy can never lead to truth. I had excellent Christian professors in history and wrote an honors thesis and my Master's thesis on Christian topics from an undisguised Christian perspective. I also studied music composition for a while, and enjoyed this greatly.

I had read much philosophy, and so the first class I took was an ethics class taught by Dr. P., who often attacked my good Christian friend and *his* fellow WSU professor, Paul Ackerman. I enrolled in this class firstly to "do battle" in the classroom as much as possible. But who was I, an amateur student of philosophy, to confront Dr. P., who had taught philosophy for years and was known on campus as a gruff militant atheist out to destroy his students' Christian faith? As I walked to the WSU campus that morning, I prayed earnestly. Our Lord's words to David from the story of David and Goliath came strongly to my mind: "I have given him into your hand." And here is what happened in that very first class.

Toward the end of the class period, Dr. P. made the statement that "ethical values are based on facts." He wrote this on the board. I raised my hand and asked: "Did you say ethical values are based on facts?" "Yes." "Could you give me an example of a fact?" He thought a moment and said, "The world is round." "And now," I asked, "would you tell me which ethical value is based on this fact?"

He was visibly stunned. The bell rang to signal the end of the class period, so he was "saved by the bell." He walked out by my side. He said, "I thought you would say somthing about religion!" (Dr. P. had heard of me as the widow of that "right wing extremist," Kenneth L. Myers, still remembered among Wichita political liberals though already deceased six years.) I replied, "That wasn't relevant then. When it is, I may say something about it."

Now, what had led me to the question was an important truth I had read in C. S. Lewis' excellent book, *The Abolition of Man.* It was that an "ought" can never be deduced from an "is." Though I didn't know it at that time, this is a well-known philosophical impasse known as "Hume's Gap," so named for the agnostic 18th-century British philosopher, David Hume. It is a hurdle no philosopher to date has overcome, for as C. S. Lewis says, "the thing is impossible." Dr. P. of course knew this, yet taught his students the opposite in the very first class of this course! The experience taught me that you must never accept at face value what an enemy of the faith says. We must verify by Scripture even the claims of purported friends of the faith, as did the Bereans with St. Paul (Acts 17:11).

Later on in the semester, Dr. P. spent almost an entire class period vilifying the Christian Church. By this time the other students, all of them of typical college age (I was in my early fifties), were used to and approved of my challenges to Dr. P. I once asked them whether they minded my frequent speaking up in classs. They told me no, on the contrary, they appreciated it, because "we often sense that what he says is wrong, but we don't know how to oppose him!" So, in this particular class, I timed Dr. P.'s diatribe against the Church. He said the church was always lagging behind the world in its ethical pronouncements. Once it had been totally opposed to divorce; now it largely accepted it. Once it had been totally opposed to abortion; now it was coming around to accepting it, and so on for issue after issue. By my watch he spent 40 minutes out of the allotted class period of 50 minutes on these arguments.

I raised my hand, and the class settled back to see the sparks fly. I said, "Dr. P., by my watch you have just spent 40 minutes running down the Christian Church. Could I please have 10 minutes for rebuttal?"

Dr. P. thought a moment, then said that we would let the class decide. He and I stepped out of the classroom. Very soon, a student came out to call us back. The class announced that they had given me 30 minutes for rebuttal!

Dr. P. asked me whether I would like to have a minister come in and give the rebuttal. I said no, because I was the one who had heard

Dr. P. speak. I might fall flat on my face with my rebuttal, but that was a risk I had to take. All this was on a Friday, so I had the weekend to prepare and pray for the next class period on the following Monday.

In essence, what I said on Monday was that the core of the issue was the definition of "Church." Yes, there were visible organizations called "churches," which might be more or less guilty of Dr. P.'s accusations. But the true "Church" was not a human organization, but rather the people of all times and places who had been regenerated in Christ. *That* Church would *never* deny God's Word and Law. True, that Church might be very small in numbers at particular times or perhaps always—only God Himself knew how many people belonged to it now or then, here or there—but that Church would always stand for biblical marriage, against abortion, and so on. When I was done, Dr. P. said, "I admit defeat."

Later on, he invited me to have conversations with him once a week on philosophy. Hoping to bring him to Christ, I accepted. These weekly conversations went on for a couple of years! He would give me books to read and critique. At times he would seemingly come cleser to Christ, but there was a pattern: he would alternately blow "hot and cold," allow room for hope and then revert to his angry atheism. Once, after the first few months of this interaction, he told me, "I thought you would give up your delusion of Christianity—you are intelligent." So he probably did all this to destroy my faith. I found out later he had interacted this way before with other Christian students. Eventually we agreed to disagree and stopped meeting.

I learned chiefly from this, but also from philosophy classes I took from other professors, that worldly philosophy—beginning with each human thinker himself—has no final answer to give to man's vital questions: Where do I come from? Where am I going? Why do I exist? How shall I live? Early on at Wichita State University I had declared a "minor" in philosophy (my "major" was and always remained my first academic love, history) but thanks to Dr. P. and other deeper looks into philosophy I cancelled that "minor." Yes, it is useful to know what goes on in that field of spiritual combat. Christians have all too often neglected to do battle there, especially for the past two or three generations. However, it has nothing to give to a Bible-believing Christian.

My experience has also been very useful in learning just how to deal with people like Dr. P. in classroom and debate. It takes courtesy, determination, diligent preparation and study, constant prayer, and also constant watchfulness for opportunities to challenge the opponent. One must be very alert and discerning to decide, with quick prayer, whether the attack before one is relatively minor and can be left unanswered for the moment, or a major onslaught that must be defended then and there. It was this kind of attack Dr. P. used in that first class I took from him, which shows that major confrontations may come quite early.

It was in 1981 that I took a class in anthropology from a lady professor, Dr. B. This was a fairly large class, perhaps 50 students. Of course the textbook was heavily permeated with Darwinian evolution, complete with "millions of years" and the amoeba-ape-man scenario. I did my best to counteract it all by asking judicious questions pointing out the very questionable origin of life from non-life in view of the law of biogenesis, the absence of transitional forms in the fossil record, and so on.

Dr. B. prided herself on being an "unbiased teacher," and therefore allowed my questions. She did her best to answer them in favor of evolution, but her best was not very convincing and she knew it. So about halfway through the course she announced that she did not seem to handle the defence of evolution very well, and she had therefore asked another professor in the WSU anthropology department, the department's expert about evolution, to visit our class and present a better case for it.

Sure enough, when the next class session began, a middle-aged, bearded man came in and spoke in favor of evolution. His presentation centered on Bernard Kettlewell's story of the British tree moth (*biston betularia*), which exists in dark and light form. According to this evolutionist "just so" story, as airborne pollution increased, tree trunks became darker as they were coated with a layer of soot. So, the light variant of the moth diminished and the dark form became predominant, allegedly because birds now had more trouble seeing the dark moths on tree trunks and ate more light moths. Then later, when pollution was alleviated, the tree trunks became lighter again, and light moths became more plentiful again as the birds ate more dark moths. This proved evolution in progress!

When he finished, I raised my hand and asked politely: "I'm sorry, I don't understand. All that seems to have happened is a change in proportion between the two forms of the tree moth which had exsisted all along. No other, higher creature seems to have evolved. How, then, does the example show evolution in progress?"

The professor became very angry! He started yelling at me that creationists always personally attacked evolutionists, and he wasn't going to stand for it! As he yelled, he noisily stomped around on the platform from which he had been speaking. He ended this outburst by stomping out of the classroom, slamming the door behind him.

I smiled, shrugged and remained silent. He had made my case for me! After the class a student came to me and said, "I had been in the middle between creation and evolution before, but after what this man said and did I have come to side with creation." A few years later, when I staffed the book table at a creation seminar with Dr. Duane Gish at Immanuel Baptist Church here in Wichita, a young man with two children came up. He said he had been a fellow student of mine in that anthropology class, and that the confrontation with the evolutionist professor had been a milestone in his own becoming a Christian. Praise our Lord!

As a postscript to the above, in 1998 came:

> the revelation that (English medical doctor Bernard) Kettlewell's argument (made in the 1950s) has not been verified by other investigators (*Nature*, vol. 396, November 5, 1998, pp. 35, 36). Furthermore, we now know that neither dark nor light moths ever spend their days on exposed tree trunks or rocks as depicted in the famous textbook pictures. His original associates have even admitted that the photographs were faked, that the moths were glued onto the tree. Thus the star witness for evolution has perjured itself, and knowledgeable evolutionists are recommending it not be used.
>
> –John D. Morris, Ph.D., in *Acts and Facts*, April 1999, Institute for Creation Research, P.O. Box 2667, El Cajon, CA 92021

As I said above, history has always been my first academic love. This goes back to my dear father who introduced me to it. How well I remember the tall bookshelves in his little study, crammed with books, mostly of history! He himself would have chosen history as his profession, perhaps to teach it at some university. His father, however, a judge in the Prussian justice administration, steered him into law.

I had a number of good teachers, but the one whom I remember first and most with thanks and respect was Dr. William Richardson, my advisor in undergraduate and later graduate studies. It was through him that I concentrated upon the study of Russian intellectual history, doing my undergraduate history honors thesis about the Old Believers (a long paper later published in full in *The Journal of Christian Reconstruction*), and my master's thesis about the "symbolist" Russian writers at the turn of the twentieth century. I saw in Dr. Richardson an excellent model of how a history teacher should be: well-informed about a wide range of subjects, organized in his class presentations, practical, fair and relevant in guidance and critique of the student's developing papers and thesis, very attentive to large and small details.

He took the trouble to teach me about style (I needed to watch my writing, still too much influenced by my background in German with its long, convoluted sentences), and even how to use commas. Last but not least, Dr. Richardson was a Christian, with the Christian's abiding respect for the truth. In that he was not alone in the department. I well remember another fine professor, Dr. Philip Thomas. Once in a conference including philosophy and history professors which I somehow attended, Dr. Thomas drily remarked about some philosophical statement, "That's all very well, but we historians pay attention to facts."

It was in 1981 that I took the anthropology class which I spoke of earlier. It met in a lecture hall in the Duerksen Fine Arts Center of Wichita State University, the location of the department of music. During that time I read Luke 19:12-27, Jesus' parable of the ten talents, and in particular about the bad servant who buried the talent he had been given in the ground. Our Lord spoke to me in my heart, "You are that servant when it comes to your music! You keep burying your music composition talent in the 'ground.' You should bring it to the 'bank' so I could receive my own with interest." "What is the 'bank' for me?" I asked. "It is the music department at WSU. Go and have your music composition evaluated." "All right," I thought, "I will."

I had had melodies sounding in my mind since I was a little child. After I started piano lessons at age 7, I began writing down some of these melodies. I wrote songs more frequently since becoming a

Christian and then only on Christian themes, but I never did much with these compositions. Ususally, I stored my compositions in a drawer in the mahogany chest in our living room.

I had just written a composition on Zephaniah 3:17: "The Lord your God in the midst of you is mighty to save. He will take great delight in you, he will rest in (or, quiet you with) His love, *He will rejoice over you with singing*." It was a most joyful, jubilant song.

The next time I got through my anthropology class, I heard His voice in me, "*Now* you go and find someone to evaluate your music!" So when class was out, I went into the hallway. I didn't even know where the Office of Musicology was! However, after a little inquiry I found it. I reached out my hand to knock at the door. Just then the door opened from the inside, and out came a nice youngish man about to leave for lunch. He looked a little like Fred Rogers on television. He introduced himself to me as Dr. M. and asked how he could help me. I instantly knew who he was: the "composer-in-residence" at WSU, well known for extremely modernistic "music." He had been a student of John Cage and he had recently composed a piece where the strings of a piano were made to howl by being strummed by combs. *Not* the teacher I would have chosen! But I knew that this was indeed the man God had chosen to be my teacher.

I explained my errand, including how Luke 19 had compelled me to come. He said, "Have you brought one of your compositions?" I hadn't. He said a little impatiently, "Can't you play a composition by heart?" So I played my "Rejoice, the Lord thy God is Singing" song. He said, "Yes, you have talent. I can't take you on in a music composition class because it is too late in the semester, but I can take you on as a private student. I am allowed eight private students, and you are the eighth."

Then he added, "Perhaps you can help me. I have been commissioned to write a symphony for the Omaha Symphony Orchestra on Creation. What biblical text would you recommend?" You may be sure I was most attentive when he mentioned the word "creation"! I asked him what texts he had been considering. He said perhaps Genesis and the Baghavad Gita (a Hindu holy book).

"Oh no, you can't!" I said. "Why not?" "Because creation is not the same in the Bible and Hinduism," I answered. "They contradict each other, and your music would show it." He became very thoughtful and said he would think this over. We arranged for my lesson schedule, and I went home.

Two days later, the phone rang. It was a friend, Sue, from out of town. "Ellen," she said, "I want you to go to WSU and talk to Dr. M.—perhaps take a course from him—you must do something for him!" "What happened?" "He was the speaker at the last meeting of a group I belong to," she answered, "He played us a tape of one of his most recent compositions. It made me so sad! He said that he had reached a dead end in his music composition. I felt a deep sadness in him. You must share your joy, the joy of the Lord, with him." "Sue," I said happily, "it has alreay happened. God is so wonderful!" And I told her how I had already met Dr. M.

Well, Dr. M. taught me for several months and became a good friend. That summer I went to Europe for a month, as I have described earlier. After my return, I went to the WSU campus on an errand and ran into Dr. M. "Come and have a cup of coffee with me in the cafeteria," he said eagerly. Of course I was glad to do this.

We sat over our cups of poor black coffee in the mostly empty cafeteria. Dr. M. told me how he had grown up in a Christian home. Then he had gone to college and lost his faith over the teaching of evolution, and also "higher criticism" of the Bible. "I was taught that the God of the Old Testament and Jesus Christ are not the same," he said, "the one is the God of wrath, the other the God of love. In order to find texts for my symphony on Creation, I read the whole Bible over again. And do you know," he said with great joy, "the God of the Old Testament is the same as the God of the New Testament!" He repeated this several times with so much joy, and I rejoiced with him. He also told me he had chosen Psalm 104 and Ezekiel 37 as texts for the symphony. (the latter being the famous Bible passage about the dry bones God brings to life again.)

The time came when his symphony was performed in Omaha. He returned and asked me whether I would like to hear it on tape. I said "Yes," with apprehension.... But, thank God, it was *good*! Later, when students performed parts of it, he gave them his testimony, much like to me in the cafeteria. What a great joy! What a wonderful God!

Always Praising Thee

IN March, 1987, Becky and I joined the wonderful church we now attend, Central Christian Church here in Wichita. The dear people took Becky to their hearts. Central offers abundant opportunities to live out our faith. I have taught Sunday school, played the piano in a nursing home and a rescue mission, and done office volunteer work with Becky for years. We have joyful, loving, and praying fellowship!

In the fall of 1987, I began to help my oldest daughter, Karen, with homeschooling her children, and have done it ever since. I have also taught many students from other homeschooling families over the years. I teach foreign languages, history, and English literature in Grades 6-12. It has been a great joy to be useful to my family. The older grandchildren have been most successful in college and graduate school. Most important, all are Christian believers, and I was able to reinforce their faith through my teaching.

In 1988 Becky helped her school (Starkey) win Third Place in a regional bowling tournament and has a big trophy to show for it!

1989 began sadly for our dear Becky. On January 17 she fell down our front steps and broke her left ankle. I was on the telephone when this happened. Becky let out a terrible scream which really alarmed me. I ran out the front door, and there was poor little Becky lying on the front sidewalk. She stopped crying and immediately got up, even though it hurt! She climbed into the Starkey school bus, and she and I thought everything would be all right. However, soon afterwards I received a phone call from Becky's school. Mrs. Gore, Becky's teacher, told Mother that Becky's ankle was swelling, and that Becky should have it X-rayed.

I quickly drove to Becky's school. Mrs. Gore, Mr. Cole, Mrs. Franklin, and another aide named Shellie came and helped Becky get into an old rickety wheelchair which had lost the rubber on one of its tires and could hardly be moved. We all were laughing! Then I drove Becky to the Wichita Clinic to have her ankle X-rayed. It turned out that Becky's fibula, a long bone in her calf, had twisted forward and pierced the skin by the ankle of her left foot, then slipped back inside.

It had also been chipped at its tip. The doctor, whose name was Dr. Robert Worsing (a funny name for a doctor!), was very nice but also very concerned. When Becky joked and said that what had happened to her was very sad, he didn't laugh! He told me that Becky would need to go to the hospital right away, and would have to have an operation at 2 p.m. that same day. She would have to have a thin steel rod inserted into her leg, and it would stay there always. But good little Becky did not cry. She was very, very brave!

Next, Becky was put into a wheelchair—this one was in perfect condition—and a nice young lady wheeled her through a very, very long underground tunnel to Wesley Medical Center. There she was admitted. Admission went fairly fast, though there were about two dozen people in line. They then brought up Becky into a hospital room on the fifth floor. Soon medical personnel came and put her on a rolling bed to bring her to the operation room on the second floor. It was now already nearly 2 o'clock. I had to leave Becky and wait in a family waiting room near the operation room. At 2:45 p.m. Dr. Worsing came and told me that everything had gone very well. The anesthesia had not made Becky sick, which was wonderful. Then after another hour or so, Becky was taken from a recovery room to her hospital room on the fourth floor of Building 4.

The next four days Becky stayed in this room. All the nurses were very good, patient and excellent caregivers. Becky loved one named Shelley the best. There were also some very nice LPN's. One was Betty, who prayed with Becky one night when her ankle really, really hurt. The nurses were very patient and always waited till Becky had said everything she wanted to say. Sometimes Becky stammered a little, but her sentences always came out perfect in the end!

Becky's greatest adventure, however, was to learn to walk with a walker. To do this she had to go to "PT"—Physical Therapy. There, a very nice young lady named Lucy helped Becky walk.

Becky was released from Wesley Hospital on January 21. Her big brother Ed helped her get from the car into the house. The next week on January 27 she went to the doctor to have her stitches taken out. Again, Becky was very brave.

There was also a BIG poster from all the kids at Starkey School which we tacked to the wall by Becky's bed. Becky cried when it arrived in the mail! She had thought she might never get to go t

Starkey again to see her friends, and never walk well again! But now she realized that she would!! There were also *many* get-well cards from Central Christian Church. Thanks be to Jesus for His healing!

In June of 1989 I gave eight programs over Christian television Channel 40 in Pittsburgh, PA. It was an exciting opportunity!

In 1991 our prayers were answered as our Becky, 21, received full-time work in the sheltered workshop of Starkey Developmental Center here in Wichita. She eventually left Starkey in 1993 due to the high bus fares and social worker fees. However, Becky does volunteer work at church and for a pro-life group two to three times weekly.

In March of 1992, I fell down the basement stairs, breaking my wrist and bruising my ribs. Several painful weeks of recovery followed.

That same year, a friend asked me to start a weekly home Bible study for another friend. There has been some turnover, but the study still continues today with about half a dozen ladies who in age could be my daughters. It is an unusual friendship circle as we come from all Christian backgrounds and originally from various different countries. Germany, Switzerland, Ecuador, Argentina, and India have all been represented. I took Titus 2:3-5 as my 'job description' for this task.

At the end of May and early June of 1994, Becky, my son Mark and his wife Debra, my son John and and his wife Patty, their children, and I had a wonderful weeklong trip to Colorado Springs and vicinity. We travelled all together in a big van. What wonderful, well-behaved children and *super* mommies! Top of Pike's Peak, Royal Gorge, Garden of the Gods, Cave of the Winds, even fishing in a pool at Canon City hotel—it was the highlight of the year. Thanks to John who planned it months in advance!

Through Central and a group it supports, International Students, Inc., I was able to reach out to foreign students at Wichita State University beginning in 1994. I have always had a great liking and interest in Chinese people, and our Lord sent us many Chinese students, including two dear young ladies from Taiwan and one from mainland China. Both students from Taiwan have become Christians and personal friends, especially our dear Gina Lin, my "daughter from Taiwan." We still have contact with and pray for her. Becky is always loving and cheerful, and all the students love her.

In August 1997, Becky, 27, received a beautiful award plaque "for endless dedication and hard work" at the Kansans for Life Banquet.

Becky and I in 1998.

In late July, 1998, Becky and I were blessed with a 1-week stay a a Salvation Army Camp for teenagers in Kansas City, where I wa invited to speak, teach an elective course, and take part in pane discussions. It was a wonderful experience which opened our eyes t the wonderful work the Salvation Army has been doing now for wel over 100 years. Its founder, William Booth, a great hero of the faith knew that to truly help the poor and needy means to give them th gospel of Jesus Christ as well as emergency food and shelter.

My family had a joyful reunion on my 75th birthday in May o 2000. Altogether, I now have 7 children, 38 grandchildren, and 4 grea grandchildren. Our Lord has kept me in good health and joyful spiri May He use me as He wills the rest of my life on earth.

Becky is now *[2000]* 30 years old, one of my greatest blessings, and I daily thank God for her. I have lost the "IQ prejudice" that I once had (thinking low IQ and mentally handicapped people are worth less than others). In this I was greatly helped by 1 Cor. 12:22: "Those parts of the body that seem to be weaker are *indispensable.*" Becky, with her total, unconditional love for everyone she meets, is a far better Christian than I. I know of at least two people she has brought to Christ, and am told our joint witness has helped many others.

I had my 40th anniversary as a Christian on July 10, 2000. It has been a wonderful, blessed life for which I thank our heavenly Father with all my heart. He has done it all so completely well in His never-failing love.

> Blessed are they that dwell in thy house; they will be always praising thee. Blessed is the man whose strength is in thee; in whose heart are thy ways. *Who passing through the valley of tears make it a well;* and the pools are filled with water. They go from strength to strength, each appears before God in Zion....O Lord of hosts, blessed is the man that trusteth in thee.

Psalm 84:4-7, 12